Come Away with Me
A Love Story
m.e. Elzey

I0630359

Dedicated to:

• • • •

Literature, films, and comedies have created characters with a facial disfigurement as a shortcut for their villains, mentally deranged psychopaths, or mockery to get a quick creep laugh. There's a simple reason producers use facial disfigurement in their work... it works.

• • • •

My wife of 52 years, our two daughters, and our five grandchildren are the most important people in my life.

• • • •

The Facial Differences and the Post Polio communities are the most resilient communities I've ever been associated with.

• • • •

Their dedication and hard work are second to none.

• • • •

Published by Little House Press

Little
House
Press, LLC

• • • •

ISBN Ebook 978-1-7379129-9-6

Chapter 1

The End

It's finally over, now I can rest.

During the late summer and throughout the autumn, I love that every evening a thick fog rolls over the city. When the slivers of light from the neon signs that adorn the streets mix with the fog, it explodes; it's like a Jackson Pollock painting that comes to life. The fusion of fog and light obscures the city streets with a cacophony of colors shooting through and reflecting off the wet city streets. It is magical.

· · · ·

She was the most beautiful woman I ever met. She had a kind of magical warmth in her presence, a light of her character. Her smile was all it took. My heart raced with fear when I first met her sitting on that bench in Homestead Park. When we had our chance meeting, it was her gentle smile that washed away my worries.

Her quick wit, fierce determination, and genuine thoughtfulness was far more important to me than how she looked, and she was beautiful. Her beauty had given her great opportunities and caused her great pain. She kept her emotional scars tucked away. What captured my heart about her was her gentle and caring soul. Despite her vulnerabilities, she was a fierce spirit, a no-nonsense woman. I still don't understand how she loved me, but I know without a doubt she did. She saw in me virtues I couldn't see or appreciate in myself. She helped me live with my demons and forgive myself.

We had both fallen victim to opposite sides of the same coin. They always made her think that her physical beauty was a stroke of luck, but the abuse by powerful men turned it into an inescapable curse. We'd fallen in love, spending long hours discussing everything and nothing. Hearing the softness of her voice, understanding her subtle wit, and understanding her vulnerabilities. I was walking to work through Homestead Park. It was a crisp fall morning when I first saw her. I remember every detail of her beautiful olive complexion, how the sun made her light brown hair sparkle, how captivating her hazel eyes were.

Standing on the sidewalk watching her every move, I still find her mesmerizing. When I realized her love for me was real, she disappeared. I watched her sitting in our regular booth. The way her delicate hands held the glass of Cabernet. She was infectious. No matter how often I dream of her, I still want more of her smile, her touch, and especially the warmth of her kiss. I love everything about her. There she is, sitting alone in our booth with a glass of Cabernet, reading the paper.

After taking a sip of wine, she folded the paper, then looked at me as if to say, 'well...get in here!'

As I entered the diner, she smiled. "Well, if it isn't Mister Jack. I was wondering if you'd make it here tonight. You realize I could see you out there on the sidewalk staring at me like some kind of pervert. You know some people could take that as a little creepy," she grinned as she poured me a glass of wine. "How did it go?"

"Time will tell, I suppose. Everything has been said and debated. I guess it's up to the stars."

"No matter what, I still feel responsible?" taking my withered left hand and kissing it.

"I agree, it was all your fault that you made me the happiest guy in the world. You're guilty of that. I wouldn't trade the time we had together for anything."

"Were you happy with your lawyer? He has a crappy reputation?"

"Yeah, he told me he had his share of enemies. In his defense, he's trying hard to contain his questionable personality. Besides, it doesn't matter he's all I can afford. I don't have a penny to my name.

Today, my lawyer did nothing but talk to the judge and to the prosecutor. Sometimes they talked in the courtroom, and other times they went to the judge's chambers. These proceedings are nothing like TV."

"That's all they did?"

"That's it."

"Jack, come away with me, we could be together again," asked Maggie as she stroked my atrophied left hand.

• • • •

"Hey Holt, get out of that bunk," said a guard as he rattled the door to my cell, waking me up.

It was near midnight at the Marsh County Detention Center. A guard leading a short man in handcuffs arrives at my cell.

"Holt, are you deaf? Wake up. Get out of that bunk. You know the routine, go to the back wall and put your nose, both hands, and your junk on the wall. Don't even think about turning around until I tell you to."

"I hear ya, boss," I answered as I glanced through the darkened cell to scc what was going on. I got out of my bunk and went to the back wall, putting my body as close to the wall as I could.

The guard opened the cell door and put the new prisoner in. "You stand right where I put you. Don't move or I'll whack you upside your head. Did you hear me?"

"Yeah, I heard you."

"Things will work out better if you follow the rules," said the guard as he closed the cell door.

"What am I supposed to do?"

"When I tell you to do something, you always answer, yes boss, no exception."

"Yes, patron."

"In English!"

"Yes, boss."

"Put your hands through the slot in the door and I'll take your cuffs off."

"Yes, boss."

The guard removed the inmate's handcuffs. "Hey Holt, you have company for a few days. You guys behave yourself. sweet dreams."

We remained quiet for a few minutes, listening to the sound of the guard's footsteps fade into the building.

My new cellmate walked toward me. "Hey man, my name is Leonardo Cota, but everyone calls me Leto." He extended his hand.

"Nice to meet you. I'm Jack Holt," I answered, noticing the grimace on his face.

"Hey brother, but what happened to your face?"

"When I was a kid, I was in a car accident and my face got banged up," I answered, sitting back on my bunk.

"That sucks!"

"Yeah, well, what are you going to do?" I answered. "I'm sorry man but I have a terrible headache."

"Are you okay?"

"I get terrible headaches. I have a big one right now."

"You should call the guard; he can help you out."

"I did, three times. They ignored all three requests,"

"Damn private prisons!"

"It will go away when I go to sleep."

"I'm tired too," answered Leto. "I'll get you some pain pills for your headache."

As soon as my head hit the pillow, I was asleep. My trial for first-degree sexual assault and first-degree murder is over. The past year has taken a toll on me.

Chapter 2

Joe Hammer

W hat was on the voicemail I just heard? Was this some kind of bad joke? I sat on the edge of my bed in my boxers and tee shirt. Again, I held the phone to my ear, wondering if I had heard it correctly. I was getting nauseated as I listened to the voicemail a second time. It was real. I stood up and took several deep breaths to calm down. Is this some kind of cruel joke? Sitting back down on the bed, I listened for the third time while taking a gulp of Pepto-Bismol.

I couldn't concentrate because I was so keyed up. Would this be an opportunity to practice law again? Did someone get wise to Eric Warren's bullshit? Did they find out he wasn't as honest as he claimed to be? I couldn't imagine the judges who disbarred me were giving me an opportunity like this. My career as one of the best prosecutors taught me to expect the unexpected. While taking a shower, I began weeping. It had been the worst two years of my life. Within a six-month period, a mix of terrible choices and internal politics had destroyed my career and my personal life. To make matters even worse, after being disbarred, my wife of fourteen years filed for a divorce, citing irreconcilable differences.

In the two years since the state judicial review board disbarred me, I had lost forty pounds, developed an ongoing upset stomach, and almost never slept through the night. It started when all five judges on the state's judiciary review board voted to disbar me.

My problems all started when Eric Warren, my boss and the District Attorney, told me he was running on a tough on crime ticket. He needed convictions, especially of a guy we could pass off as a major kingpin in the local gangs that perpetuate our drug problem, a guy that was suspected of being a drug dealer. Then, as luck would have it, there was Miguel Acosta, the perfect made to order bad guy. He was covered with second-rate tattoos and had a record of

7

petty crimes starting when he was an eight-year-old kid. The media would jump on this like flies on a pile of crap. There was only one problem. He was innocent, and I knew it! I could have done the honorable thing and told the lawyer for the defense, but I didn't. I used my privilege as a white prosecutor by focusing on his looks alone. Why not? The local media would do my job for me. And why not? My thinking back then was that Acosta was no doubt guilty of something and, frankly, society was better off with him behind bars. Acosta pled guilty and agreed to twenty years in prison. I got the conviction the DA needed to help his reelection bid as a tough on crime, district attorney. Six months later, a paralegal proved I had withheld evidence that would have exonerated Miguel Acosta. Eric Warren denied having any knowledge of my actions. To illustrate his commitment to the rule of law. The DA petitioned the judicial review board to disbar me. It was the most humiliating moment in my life. It was especially painful since one judge on the judiciary panel, Judge William Horton, was my former mentor. Working for the judge was my first job out of law school. Twenty-one years later, my former mentor voted to disbar me. The event destroyed not only my confidence, but my entire life.

Losing my license to practice law was the most horrible thing that ever happened to me. The worst part was I deserved it. My string of self-inflicted bad luck was far from over. Only three weeks after being disbarred, my wife not only filed for divorce, but she also hired my nemesis, a divorce lawyer named Penelope Bergdorf. Bergdorf was the best-connected lawyer in the city. She was long past being a talented lawyer. Somehow, she knew every woman with whom I'd had an extramarital affair. During the divorce negotiations, Penelope made it impossible for me to argue my side of the story. I had no choice but to agree to the terms she dictated. I lost everything but five thousand dollars and a sixteen-year-old rusted-out Dodge Durango. As awful as the divorce was, it wasn't a surprise, since I had never been faithful. I spent the next two years trying to figure out what to do with the rest of my life. Cheap whisky didn't help ease my pain. In time, I learned to accept my lot and start building a new life. Inquiring with several law firms, I learned that not only am I a disbarred lawyer, but a pariah

When I woke up, I stared at the phone, trying to remember if I had checked my voicemail from the night before. Still in my boxers, I checked on the chance that someone might have called. To my surprise, there was one new message. It was from Becky McCarthy, Judge William Horton's assistant. She asked if I could call her at my earliest convenience. She left her direct phone number. What could my former boss and onetime mentor want? As I got ready for work, I kept speculating about why Judge Horton's assistant would be calling. Later, while on my morning break at the home improvement center, I returned her call.

· · · ·

"Hello, Judge Horton's office. How can I help you?" answered Becky McCarthy.

"This is Joe Hammer. I'm returning your phone call."

"Hello Mr. Hammer. How are you this morning?"

"I'm fine, thank you. How are you?"

"Doing well, thanks. The reason I called is Judge Horton, and the judiciary panel reinstated you to the bar. Meaning you'll be able to practice law again. Are you interested in practicing law again?"

"I don't know what to say. You bet I'm interested." I cleared my throat, trying my best not to sob on the phone.

"Mr. Hammer, just so you know there are a few caveats with this reinstatement. Judge Horton can explain that when you see him. Can you meet him tomorrow at the Old Union Club at 4:00PM?"

"Yes, of course I can meet him," I answered. We talk for a few more minutes before hanging up.

Anxiety soon crept in. Why would they vote to reinstate me to the bar? I became obsessed with why Judge Horton changed his mind. What happened? Did they figure out that Eric Warren set me up? Wouldn't that be great? I'd love to see that son-of a-bitch go to prison, especially after the crap he pulled on me. My mind kept playing these situations over and over.

· · · ·

I arrived at the Old Union Club fifteen minutes early. Over the past twenty-four hours, I went over every conceivable scenario for why the judge reinstated me to the bar. By the time I parked the car, I began having difficulty breathing. I sat in my car taking deep breaths, trying to calm my nerves. A feeling of tranquility settled within me, which helped me to meet my old mentor. I walked into the half-light of the Old Union Club a few minutes early. I hadn't slept since I had heard the news from the judge's assistant. The time had arrived to meet my mentor, Judge William Horton, face to face. The place looked much the same as I remember back when I was a clerk for the judge.

I introduced myself to the receptionist, who was expecting me. She escorted me to a small private meeting room where Judge Horton waited.

"Would you like anything to drink?" she asked.

"A glass of water would be fine."

"I'll bring it to you."

Just off the public lounge were small, private meeting rooms where people could talk. She opened the door and extended her arm, inviting me to enter.

It took me back to when I first worked for Judge Horton. He had become an elderly man. He stood up with the help of a cane. I had forgotten his smile until that moment. It reminded me of how kind he was as a person and as a judge. He was fair-minded, dedicated to the rule of law, and straightforward with issues of the law. Most smart lawyers heeded the judge's not too subtle advice.

"I'll be right back with your water, Mr. Hammer," said the woman as she closed the door behind her.

"It's good to see you again. Thank you for this opportunity," I said, extending my hand.

The judge shook my hand, smiled, and while taking his seat again, "Please have a seat, Joe. I've been looking forward to seeing you again. You're looking good."

"Thank you, you're looking good yourself. How have you been?"

"I'm doing fine, thank you," answered the judge as he took a drink of scotch. He stared at me as if he were studying. "What have you been doing since we disbarred you?"

"Surviving."

"I heard your wife divorced you. Is that true?"

"Yeah, she sure did."

"Remind me. Did you have any kids?"

"No, no kids, Your Honor."

"Sounds like you've been having a tough time. How long has it been since you lost your license?"

"Almost two years."

"It's been a while, huh," said the judge, taking another drink of scotch. "You seem more unassuming than you used to be."

"The past couple of years have been a humbling experience. On top of being disbarred, my wife filed for divorce. All of this in a six-month period."

"I suppose that would knock the wind out of your sails. Well, Joe, who knows, maybe something good will come from your experience. I suspect you didn't come here to chitchat. We'd better get down to business. When you clerked for me, you had the potential of being one fine lawyer. The fact is Joe; you didn't take advantage of everything you worked for. You squandered everything for petty office politics and feeding your ego," said Judge Horton.

"I understand."

"When I brought up reinstating you to the bar, the four other judges on the judiciary panel didn't like the idea. The rules set up to reinstate a lawyer is by a simple majority. I needed two other judges to vote to reinstate you. It took a little arm twisting, but I prevailed with a three to two vote."

"I appreciate what you've done."

"You were and still are, a wonder. It's surprising that someone you've belittled along the way didn't take you out behind the barn and beat the crap out of you. It would have taken you down and made you humble. The fact is Joe; you like many other conscientious hard-working men and women you were damn good but being good at something doesn't give you a license to be so disagreeable. Make no mistake Joe, you have a distasteful personality. I just reviewed the evidence in your disbarment and it's obvious the DA's motion to disbar you was correct. You ignored evidence and sent an innocent man to prison. It looks like Mr. Acosta's public defender failed his client. I did some checking, and the defense attorney for the public defender's office had eighty-two open cases. Our judicial system failed Mr. Acosta. You discredited all prosecuting attorneys by your illegal prosecution to bolster the DA's reelection bid. We knew Eric's reputation when we reviewed his petition to have you disbarred. We also knew your reputation. I'm giving you an opportunity to redeem yourself. Joe, I'll be honest, for me disbarring you was easy, you broke the public trust and committed an illegal act. Our system is at fault. The legal system denied Mr. Acosta due process. He was the low hanging fruit that would most certainly get Eric Warren reelected. All lawyers do the best they can to pursue justice. You built your career by prosecuting many people who lacked the resources to defend themselves. With no hesitation, you identified them as the leeches of our society. Prosecuting those individuals who had no chance of receiving a fair trial, you displayed an excessive amount of pride. Your job was to protect our society by pursuing justice. Instead, you played politics to boost your ego. You used those who had no ability to fight back to inflate your convictions record. Counting convictions was much more important than serving justice. Let's be clear, you got disbarred because you're a top-notch prick."

It was hard listening to the judge especially since everything he said was true. I had never had someone so calm and collected as Judge Horton tell me what a son-of-a-bitch I was.

"Joe, besides being a prick, we also knew that Eric Warren played to your big ego and set you up. There was a paralegal you didn't even know who despised you so much she risked her future to report you to the authorities. If you're looking for someone to blame for the mess you've been in, look in the mirror."

"I understand."

Judge Horton took a sip of scotch, took a deep breath, "I was curious why the DA's office didn't bring criminal charges against you. A few months after we disbarred you, I asked a confidant to do a little undercover investigation. I wanted to know how many of the cases you prosecuted did the DA's office investigate. My confidant came back and said the DA's office had not investigated a single case you had prosecuted. That was extraordinary. If you were prosecuting people to further your own career, that's bad. It's so bad that disbarring you would have been the least of your problems. The DA's office had a legal obligation to charge you with prosecutorial misconduct."

"I don't understand?"

"All Eric did was to file an ethics motion with us to have you disbarred. It's reasonable to assume the DA would form a task force to investigate the cases you handled over your twenty-year career.

The DA's office didn't investigate a single case you prosecuted. Joe, now's the time to come clean. How many times did you prosecute an innocent man?"

"Prior to Miguel Acosta, I'd done nothing illegal," I answered. "I admit my personality was terrible. I also admit that I deserved everything I got. Please believe me, I never broke the oath of my office before Mr. Acosta's case."

"Maybe had you been more professional one of your colleagues would have told you about Eric Warren. Do you remember a guy named Carlo Ricci?"

"I think I do. That's not the answer you're looking for." I answered, squinting my eyes, trying to figure out why that name sounds so familiar.

"Let me know if you remember if you remember this Carlo guy," asked the judge.

"Can you tell me why I should know him?"

"In time. That's all I can say," responded the judge.

"May I ask you something?"

"Of course."

"What I don't understand is why are you reinstating me?"

"Joe, I have some unfinished business. If you keep your mouth shut and practice law, you'd be a lawyer. Listen to me Joe, you don't deserve a second chance. You're an end to a means. Do you want to practice criminal law?"

"It's all I know."

"Is that a, yes?"

"Yes, sir, I want to practice criminal law."

"Good. Here's what you will do. I will sponsor you for the next year. You will do what I tell you with no questions asked. Make no mistake, you're on probation. Starting tomorrow, you'll start working for the Marsh County public defender's office. You'll be working for Jackie Goldman. Do you know her?"

"No, I don't believe so."

"Well, she knows you all too well. Three times she refused my request to assign you to work for her. I told her that if you got out of line, I would get involved. She's one sharp lawyer who has her hands full."

"May I ask you something?"

"Sure."

"Did you find anyone who liked me or at least respected me?"

"No, your reputation precedes you. I'm afraid you have a lot of work to do in that regard."

"Okay."

"Let's move on, Joe. You'll work for the public defender's office, but you'll have only one client, a man named Jack Holt. He is the perfect example of a person our judicial system has failed. Police arrested him for first-degree murder and first-degree sexual assault. The public defender's office sent a new lawyer to represent him through the arraignment. The judge ruled there was enough evidence to hold him over for trial. He set bail at one million dollars. The high bail set means he's sitting in the Marsh County Detention Center until trial. The homicide detectives have yet to interrogate him."

"What's the problem?"

"I don't know. You need to find out for yourself."

"Why is this guy my only client?"

"Like I said, I have unfinished business." Answered Judge Horton.

Chapter 3

Janet Fischer, Jury Foreperson.

My jaw dropped in disbelief when I learned I was one of the fortunate fourteen selected to serve on a jury. It was especially worrisome to be on a jury, deciding the fate of a man charged with the rape and murder of a woman. Thank God we don't have capital punishment in this state anymore. Working at Santa Rosa's Children's Hospital caring for terminally ill children. It sounds odd, I know, but I look at what I do as a service to the surviving family members. No child should ever die, but they do. By the time I care for these poor children, several doctors have agreed that there is no hope. Part of my job is to provide a comfortable death to a child ravaged by a ruthless disease. The other part is to provide moral support for the grieving family. I have to be strong even when the circumstances are hard to accept.

Before being notified that I was on jury duty, I'd never stepped foot in a courtroom. The difference between television lawyers and real-life lawyers is astonishing. There were times it was hard to stay awake when the lawyers and the judge were discussing some meaningless procedure or a particular point of law.

There were fourteen of us jurors selected to hear the trial of Jack Holt. When the trial concluded, the judge thanked the alternate jurors for their service before a bailiff escorted them from the courtroom.

"The fate of the defendant is now in your hands," said the judge as she began giving the jury their instructions. "Next to voting, serving on a jury is the most important responsibility of a citizen in our democracy. We have heard witnesses from both the prosecution and the defense. You have seen all the evidence. Now it is up to you to decide whether Mr. Holt is guilty or innocent, based on the trial testimony and evidence. To find Mr. Holt guilty of these charges, you must believe he is guilty beyond any reasonable doubt. Facts are open to many interpretations, as you will discover during your deliberations. Being part of this process can be one of the most taxing situations in your life. You are adults, and I expect you to conduct yourself as adults during the deliberation. Remember, you are deciding the fate of an individual. Take your responsibilities serious. To convict Mr. Holt of these charges, you must all agree that he is guilty beyond any reasonable doubt. If there is any question about his guilt, you must acquit." The judge looked at me. "Are you Janet Fischer?"

"Yes."

"Mrs. Fischer, I'm assigning you as the foreperson."

"I appreciate the offer, but Your Honor," I responded, "I would rather not be the foreperson."

"Mrs. Fischer, it is not an offer," said the judge as she considered her words. "I assigned you to be the foreperson. I expect you to show leadership and direct this jury to a verdict."

"Your Honor, please, I'm not trying to be difficult, but I do not know what to do."

The judge gazed at me for what seemed to be an eternity. "You'll do an excellent job, Mrs. Fischer," she responded, then looked at the jury. "One last word before I put this trial in your hands. A hung jury is unacceptable. More often than not, it is the failure of one or two people. If each of you recall, when we started the jury selection process, I asked each of you if you could convict a person of these serious charges. All of you said you would have no problem convicting if the evidence proved their guilt beyond a reasonable doubt. This, ladies and gentlemen, is serious business, and again I'll underscore that I expect you to conduct yourselves in good faith."

Why the hell did she select me to be the jury foreperson? I'm not even sure what the person does. Is it foreman, forewoman, or foreperson? Ah God, help me; why did she choose me? I can't believe it.

After the bailiff explained what a foreperson did, I did not want the job. The bailiff explained the judge selected me for a reason; he doubted she would change her mind. I'm stuck!

I don't handle conflict very well. It's something I'm not good at and avoid at all costs. I'm worried about two jurors. One man is irritating. I think his name is Henry Keller. The intensity of his scowl reveals the anger he harbors towards the world. When the trial broke for lunch, he always shared his opinion. I think he had found the defendant guilty the moment he saw him. Although I've never discussed this guy with anyone, I suspect the other jurors don't care for him either. Most of the things he says are offensive.

There's a woman who seems to always be in a hurry and appears to get annoyed at some other jurors. I'm not sure how I will deal with their horrible personalities. One bailiff suggested everyone wear a nametag. He assured me he'd be there if things got too intense. I wasn't sure what he meant by that remark, and I wasn't sure I wanted to know. I guess what will happen will happen.

Chapter 4

The Jury

Two bailiffs escorted us to the eighth-floor jury room. It is part of a suite comprising the courtroom, the judge's chambers and her staff, and the jury room. The jury room itself is rectangular with the entrance at the northeast corner of the room. There are five enormous windows on the south wall with a panoramic view of the city. The forested foothills in the southern part of Marsh County are off in the distance. It has a large wooden table with twelve wooden chairs, five on each side and one at each end. Two ceiling fans silently moved the air.

A hallway was on the west side of the jury room. It leads to a small kitchenette on the left, a closet on the right, and two unisex restrooms at the end of the short hallway.

After the bailiffs escorted us to the jury room, they took a roll call to make sure everyone was present and accounted for. Afterward, the older bailiff began giving instructions.

"Just a few rules Judge Taylor wants us to share with you. First, my name is Gus, and my partner is Dennis. During deliberations, Dennis and I will sit just outside the door if you have questions or special needs that come up. There will be a roll call every time the jury breaks and reconvenes. If there are any smokers on the jury, you cannot smoke in the jury room that includes the two restrooms and the kitchenette. If you need to have a smoke, let Dennis know and he will take you to the designated smoking area in the parking garage. Keep in mind that you cannot stop the deliberations to have a smoke. You can smoke before we start in the morning, during a break, or after deliberations. Dennis will escort you if time permits. Dennis will collect all smart phones, pads, or computers not allowed during deliberations. Before Dennis takes your electronics, please make sure the devices are off. While he's collecting your phones, pads, or computers, I'll answer questions."

"When Judge Taylor said a hung jury was unacceptable," asked Henry Keller. "How are we supposed to take that statement?"

"Well," the bailiff smiled, "I would take everything the judge says seriously. Let me put it this way: I would not go to the judge and tell her you have a hung jury. That would be a terrible idea. Any more questions?" Gus looks around the jury room. "Okay then, I think we're done here." The bailiff looked at me. "Madam foreperson, if you'll be so kind to sit here at the head of the table. All right, thank you for your time and good luck."

Dennis, the other bailiff, looked at everyone. "Has everyone given me his or her phone, pad, or computer?" He waited for a few seconds. "Okay, then I think we're done here. Your phones are in safekeeping until you've finished."

I asked the bailiff if I could get some nametags and some black markers. I took his advice and asked everyone to wear a nametag, at least for the first few hours. We'd been together for six days, but it wasn't the best environment to promote interaction. Gus returned with nametags and felt markers. He reminded me they'd be just outside the door if I needed anything. He winked.

While Gus was giving his instructions, a cafeteria worker rolled a cart into the kitchenette. He set up two containers of coffee, hot water, various tea bags, a few soft drinks, water, plus cookies.

After the cafeteria worker and the bailiffs had gone, I took my seat at the head of the table. Deciding someone's fate still troubled me, but I'm determined to do my best, regardless of the verdict.

As the other jurors were getting an afternoon snack and coffee, I watched as the clear sky give way to the dark stormy clouds rolling in from the west. The weather was becoming darker and more ominous. I feared the worst was yet to come.

It was time to decide the fate. "If I can have everyone's attention for a second," I said as I stood up, "we need to get started. How about everyone writes his or her first name on a label, then put it on your shirt or blouse? On that note, could everyone please take their seats in the next couple of minutes? We need to get going."

To calm myself down, I drew a rectangle that represented the jury table. As each person took a seat, I numbered their location by where I sat, making myself juror number one. A middle-aged black woman, Sara King, with a beautiful smile, sat to my immediate left. She was juror number two. Next to Sara was a man named Henry Keller, juror number three. Next to Henry was a man named Marty Chu, juror number four. Mike Shepard, juror #5, sat on the other side of Marty. The chair on the other side of Mike Shepard was empty. Whoever sat here would-be juror number six. A large, buxom thirty something black woman named Kayla, juror number seven, sat on the other end of the table opposite me. To Kayla's left were Hassan Saragana, juror number eight. Alexandro Molino number nine, Oscar Rosenthal number ten, Ira McMillian number eleven, and Michael Eckert juror number twelve. I had all but one person's name on my hand-drawn chart. Linda Sawyer would return from the restroom to take the vacant seat.

"Hello, my name is Oscar," said an older man as he reached for a label and a felt marker.

"Nice to meet you. My name is Ira McMillian," answered the man as he took a label. "When you're done, could I use your marker?"

"Sure, give me a second."

A juror named Mike Shepard grabbed a few labels and a marker and took them to where he was sitting and put them in the middle of the table.

Linda Sawyer took her seat next to Mike Shepard. "What's with the label?"

"The foreperson suggested we write our name on the nametags and put them on our shirt. I'm Mike Shepard."

"That's nice," she responded as she looked at me. "Are you serious? Why?"

Kayla Rooney raised her eyebrows.

"It was just a suggestion," I answered. "What's your name?"

"I'm Linda Sawyer. I paid four hundred dollars for this blouse and there's no way in hell I'm putting a sticky label on it."

"That's fine," I answered as I wrote her name. "Like I said, it was just a suggestion."

I noticed Kayla Rooney sitting on the other side of Linda at the end of the table, making another face. Kayla leaned over to feel the fabric. "Did you really pay that much?"

"What are you doing?"

"I was feeling your fabric. Sweetheart, not to hurt your feelings, but if you paid four hundred bucks for that blouse, you got ripped off."

"Who the hell do you think you are?"

"I'm Kayla Rooney. Not to hurt your feelings, but girl, you're a big-time bullshit artist or that store saw you coming. What did you say your name was?"

"I'm Linda Sawyer," she answered, then turned her back toward her.

"Could I have the marker, your majesty?" asked Kayla. "I will put my name on the label and stick it on the eighteen-dollar blouse from Target."

She slides the marker to Kayla without turning around.

• • • •

"Was there rain in the forecast?" asked Marty Chu as he stared out of the window.

"I never watch the local news," answered Henry Keller, standing on the left side of Marty.

"I watched the weather forecast before coming in this morning. This front will be here for a couple more days," responded a juror who was standing to the right of Marty. "My name is Hassan Saragana."

"Nice to meet you," answered Marty as they shook hands.

Henry Keller looks at Hassan, "Paki?"

I could see Henry's one-word comment surprised both Hassan and Marti. Both men grinned. Oh God, Henry has already started.

"Des Moines," Hassan replied.

"Where are your parents from?" asked Henry.

Hassan smiles. "Both of my parents were born and raised in Des Moines," he answered. "Thank you for your interest in my family tree. I guess we'd better go sit down, we're almost ready to start."

"If everyone could please take their seats, we need to get started as soon as possible," I said.

"Come on, everyone, let's get moving," ordered Linda Sawyer. "Some of us have lives. Move it!"

"Excuse me," I said. "What was your name again?"

"Linda."

"I appreciate your help, Linda, but I can handle it. Thank you."

"Well, get your act together," answered Linda. "Some of us have lives to get back to."

"Damn girl," said Kayla with a slight grin and raised eyebrows. "Did you get up on the wrong side of the bed or what?"

"You know you'd be better off if you'd just keep your comments to yourself," Linda responded.

Kayla grinned. "Or what? You didn't finish."

"You know what I mean."

"Here's something to consider. Don't you dare talk to me the way you just talked to the foreperson?"

Linda Sawyer's verbal exchange that was taking place before we'd even started surprised me. I decided I had to redirect Linda and Kayla. "Since we're all here and I'm new at being the foreperson, are there any suggestions? I'm open to any ideas," asked Janet.

"This case is a straightforward decision," said Henry. "I say we vote and get this nonsense over with so we can go home."

"That's an outstanding idea," said Linda. "I second that motion. Let's vote right now."

"My name is Alex, and I think we owe it to Mr. Holt to at least have a conversation about his guilt or innocence. We should discuss the merits of the charges against Mr. Holt. He could spend the rest of his life behind bars without the possibility of parole."

"I agree with Alex. We should at least review the case to be sure nothing is overlooked," said Oscar Rosenthal.

"I think it's a waste of time to go over the circumstances of a case we just heard," said Michael Eckert. "Let's vote and see what happens."

"I think a vote would tell us where we all stand," said Hassan Saragana. "If we all vote the same way, then we've saved a lot of time. If we have different opinions, then we can discuss the details of the trial."

"We should talk about the case before we vote," said Sara King, sitting to my left. "We're here to decide if the prosecution proved beyond a reasonable doubt. Did Jack Holt rape and murder Maggie Stewart? Some of you want to be expedient and take a vote. We are discussing a man's life we should discuss the case before voting."

"We should vote on where we go from here. Those of you who want to have a vote right now without discussing the case, please raise your hand."

The jury voted ten to two to take a vote and see what happens.

"It looks like we will have a vote. The next question is whether it's a secret ballot or do we go around the table and everyone announces their vote? Let's have a show of hands for those in favor of a secret ballot." No one was in favor of a secret ballot. "Here's what we will do. I will start with Sara on my left and go around the table and ask each one of you for your decision. Unless there's an objection, let's start."

Chapter 5

Jack Holt

"**H**ey vato, how come they brought you back so late?" asked my new cellmate Leto.

"The trial was late getting out and the shuttle that brings me back here was late. I had to wait at the holding cell at the courthouse. I'm starting to think my convenience isn't of their priorities."

"How'd the trial go?"

"Ugh, today, the lawyers argued over a bunch of issues. They'd talk in the courtroom for a few minutes, then they'd go to the judge's chambers for a while. It's amazing anything gets done."

"How is the lawyer from the public defender's office doing for you?"

"It doesn't matter?" I answered. "He's the only lawyer I could afford, and he's free. If it wasn't for the public defender's office, I'd be out of luck."

"Do you like the guy they got for you?"

"Yeah, he's okay. I'm his only client. They just let him practice law again. I'm sort of his guinea pig. I guess he's doing the best he can. What do I know?"

"The lawyer they assigned to me looks like a boy scout. I will spend the rest of my life in jail because I sold a little pot to a freckle face kid from the suburbs. I might ask for your lawyer if he gets you off. Now that I think about it, if you go to prison, well... I don't think I'll ask for him."

"Hey man, I'd like to talk, but I'm tired as hell."

"Before you check out, I want to apologize to you for my reaction to your face. I felt bad all day long. I got to thinking about your face when I realized you shouldn't feel bad about it. Let's face it Jack, I doubt you would have been all that good looking, anyway."

Jack sat up in his bunk. "Excuse me?"

"I was serious about the apology. The rest I was pulling your leg," Leto said with a grin. "Now I'm being serious. I have a gift for you."

"Oh, yeah?"

"You said last night that you had a headache. It turns out it's easier to get shit in here than on the outside." Leto walks to the front of the cell and looks in both directions. "I got twenty brown sugar pills that will help you with your headaches."

"Brown sugar? What are you talking about?"

"Hold on, vato," Leto once again checked the cellblock. "It's a pill made from a diluted heroin. Only take half a pill, it will take care of your pain and make you sleep like a baby."

"Is it safe?"

"It's heroin. What do you think? If you only take half a pill, it will help with your pain and let you sleep. Don't take an entire pill or you'll get knocked on your ass. If you take two, you'll get knocked on your ass forever."

"How much do I owe you?"

"It's on me," answered Leto.

"Seriously?"

"Nah man, they're on the house, but be careful don't over-do it with these pills. Okay?"

"Thanks, man," answered Jack. "Are these pills addictive?"

"Oh yeah, man, but not if you only take half a pill. Only take these pills when you're in pain. If you do more, the brown sugar pills are not only addictive, but they will also put your ass in an early grave."

I put the half pill on my tongue and took a drink of water. In seconds, I felt a soothing sensation throughout my body. Like a warm blanket. Oh, man, I haven't slept like this in a long time.

• • • •

A s usual, I'm walking to work through Homestead Park. There's a chilly fall snap in the air. As I walk over a footbridge, I notice a woman sitting on a park bench near the bank of the North Fork River. She doesn't look good. What happened? I kept a close eye on her. You never know what creeps are in a park like this. I watch as she attempts to get up. Should I go see if she's, okay? Then she makes another attempt to stand up only to fall back on the bench in slow motion. She looks a little drunk.

Homestead Park is a four-hundred-acre tree-covered park in the center of the city. It's a hub for the surrounding community. It has a two-mile workout trail where people can do calisthenics or sit on one of the park's many benches and take it all in. The North Fork River, a medium-sized creek, meanders through the center of the park on its way to join the Little Blue River. The park has old-growth oak, sugar maple, walnut, hickory, and poplar trees. There are ramadas complete with concrete picnic tables and barbecue pits.

I pay attention to the woman on the park bench. Should I stick my nose in her business? I don't want to frighten her. As I watch, she makes her third attempt to stand. She loses her balance, and once again falls back on the bench. I look around to see if there's anyone who can help this woman. I can't see anyone in the park. Something isn't right. I can't leave her until I know she's okay. Damn! I have to see what's going on with her. I'd feel better if there was a park ranger around. Where are those guys when you need them? I cross the wooden footbridge, get off the trail and approach her, stopping a good twenty feet away.

"Are you okay?"

"Mr. Jack; don't you recognize me?" answered Maggie. "You're having a dream, Jack."

"Oh yeah, what's going on? I keep forgetting. Everything seems so real."

"Mr. Jack, come sit next to me. I can't tell you how much I miss you."

"Maggie, I would give anything to be with you again."

She smiled and caressed the atrophied left hand. "I've missed you. Did you know you're the love of my life?"

"Can I give you a kiss?"

"Sure, you can, silly," Maggie answered with her smile. "Do you know what they call a bunch of kisses?"

"Beats me. What do they call a bunch of kisses?"

"A slobber of smooches. Hey, that's a fact, look it up. It's your dream. You can kiss me all you like."

She had a black eye, and the right side of her face looked swollen. "How did you get those black and blue bruises on your face?"

"This is your dream of when we first met. I lied to you and told you I fell on a morning jog."

"Why did you lie to me?"

"Why should I have told you? I didn't know who you were. It made no sense to tell you that my sorry excuse of a husband hit me."

"Why?"

"He wanted total control over me. He wanted total control of my money. The bastard got mad at me when I told him there was nothing I could do. That was kind of true, but I used that excuse to not let him get anywhere near my money. I didn't trust that greedy control freak. That's water under the bridge. Tell me how your trial is going?"

"My lawyer thinks the prosecution has a weak case and that I'll get off. I think the detectives and the prosecutor thought I was guilty as soon as they saw my face. Their entire case revolves around the fact I refused to talk to the detectives until I had a lawyer. Their subtle claim is that no woman as beautiful as you would have sex with me. That's their case. Can you believe that? I'm not as optimistic as my lawyer."

Maggie looked into my eyes. I noticed a tear going down her cheek. "I'm sorry you're going through this. It's not right. I wish there was something I could do."

"There is something you can do if you'd like?"

"What?"

"Considering it's my dream and we're sitting on the bank of this beautiful creek. Let's just sit here and be with each other."

"I think that's a dandy idea. Let's do that," answered Maggie as she took my left hand and rested her head on my shoulder. We sat all morning taking in the park's beauty.

Chapter 6

Joe Hammer

It was as if I had a terrible hangover. I had a headache, my stomach was full of butterflies, and my eyes were bloodshot. I grabbed a bottle of Pepto-Bismol from the nightstand and took a gulp. All night, my mind raced from one thought to another. I reviewed my conversation with Judge Horton. Everything that happened over the past two years has been on my mind. My concern about paying the bills stemmed from my uncertainty about how much I would make as a public defender. I blamed Penelope Bergdorf, my wife's divorce lawyer. I knew I had it coming, yet I was obsessed about how she destroyed me during the divorce. She made sure everyone knew how much of an unbelievable womanizer I'd been.

Once again, I contemplated giving up practicing law. I thought I might move to a part of the country where no one knew me. I could do something else for a living. Was I nothing more than a vulgar, over educated windbag? Everything Judge Horton and Penelope Bergdorf had said to me was long overdue and personal. I sent an innocent guy to prison, only to kiss Eric's ass and improve my career objectives. The judge forced me to admit, if only to myself, that for twenty years I'd been offensive to many people. It was apparent that all of my problems were self-inflicted.

Throughout the night, I wondered why I was representing only one client. It made little sense to have all my years of experience defending one man. What was so special about this Jack Holt guy? Why did he merit all this attention?

Between obsessing about everything, I got ready for my first day on the job with the public defender's office. I sat at my dining table wondering if I was doing the right thing by getting back into the game. Despite my continual second-guessing of their motives, I began planning my day. I had a nine AM appointment to meet my new boss, Jackie Goldman, at the Marsh County Public Defender's office.

Since I only had one client, I wanted to find out as much as I could from the DA's office. To get the process started, I called Claudia Spurlock, one of the District Attorney's administrative assistants. I knew without a doubt that I had a wonderful relationship with Claudia, and she could give me some insight about my client.

"Good morning," Claudia answered in her usual pleasant voice. "This is the District Attorney's office. How may I help you?"

"Hello Claudia, this is Joe Hammer. How are you today?"

"What do you want?" she asked. "You're not coming back to work here, are you? God help us if you are!"

That is definitely the warm greeting I expected. "I'm just trying to find out who's prosecuting a man named Jack Holt."

"I thought they disbarred you?"

"Yeah, they did, but I'm back practicing law in the public defender's office. Jack Holt is my client."

"Does this Jack Holt guy know what a total creep you are?"

"Claudia, could you tell me who's prosecuting Mr. Holt?"

"Jackson Maynard extension 5488."

"Is he in the office?"

"Why don't you dial his extension and find out," answered Claudia, "I think we're done here." The line went dead.

This is not the least bit fun, I thought to myself as I dialed Jackson's direct number.

"This is Jackson Maynard; how can I help you?"

"Hello Jackson, this is," he cut me off.

"So, it's true, those old men on the judiciary review board let you practice law again. Wow, that's incredible."

"Yeah, well, what can I say? It seems they did. How have you been, Jackson?"

"What do you want?" he asked, ignoring my question.

"I understand you're handling the Jack Holt prosecution. Is that correct?"

"Yeah."

"Can I drop by this afternoon and get his file? I'd like to get up to speed on what's going on with him."

"We don't do that anymore. The county installed a new system after the judges disbarred you. Give me your email. I'll have the tech people set you up to get data from our office and coroner's office. That only takes a few minutes, then you can download everything we have on your client. Talk to the detectives. They're a little pissed."

"I was planning on doing that, thanks."

"FYI, they're pissed at your client."

"Oh yeah. What about?"

"Your client refused to talk to them even before he was a suspect. This guy has his head up his ass. I almost forgot you can access the autopsy reports online too. When you read the autopsy report, you'll know why he is going away for a long time."

"Thanks, Jackson."

"What law firm are you with, or are you on your own?"

"I'm with the public defender's office. In fact, I just started today."

"So poetic justice exists, and you're a shining example of it. I have to admit, Joe, you would have been a good lawyer if you weren't such a miserable son-of-a-bitch."

"Jackson, what can I say?"

"Joe, all I can say is you have your work cut out for you with this Holt character. This guy is as guilty as they come. Your client makes me have second thoughts about the state legislature doing away with the death penalty. That bastard is guilty and deserves a needle in his arm."

After my encounter with Claudia Spurlock and my brief conversation with Jackson Maynard, I once again started having doubts about my new law career. Grabbing my bottle of Pepto-Bismol and took a drink.

. . . .

I made my way through a light drizzle in the morning's city traffic to meet my new supervisor, Jackie Goldman, arriving twenty-minutes early.

Restarting your profession under any circumstances is difficult. It was even more difficult to start the next chapter of my legal career in the public defender's office. I had become well-known for criticizing their lawyers. They were the lowest of the low in the legal profession, even lower than ambulance chasers. There was no respect on my part for the liberal lawyers who worked there, as they were nothing but pansy asses. I believed most of them wouldn't know good legal work if their life depended on it. I knew when competing with a so-called lawyer from the public defender's office, a conviction was in the bag. The defendant would accept a plea deal, based on the advice of their public defender, who had limited knowledge of their client. Working as a grunt lawyer in the public defender's office was a tough pill to swallow. It was time to suck it up, swallow my pride, and get to work if I wanted to practice law again. The fact is, I never had much respect for private practice defense lawyers either. I thought they overcharged their clients for mediocre representation.

After finding out the elevator was out of order, I walked up three flights of stairs to the public defender's office. It surprised me to discover the office needed repair. A third of the cardboard ceiling tiles were missing, exposing the dark void of wiring and pipes that worked their way above the stained ceiling tiles. The Herman Miller office cubicles were old and sometimes held in position by worn-out bookcases beaming with long-forgotten files and briefs.

Every year Jackie Goldman negotiated with the Governor's office, Marsh County, and the city to increase the operating budget, and every year the budget was smaller. Because of inadequate funding from Marsh County and the state, the Public Defender's office could not cover the legal fees for defending its clients. The public defender's office was an afterthought to the state, county, and city officials. The only positive thing about the public defender's office was its proximity to the Marsh County courthouse, only two blocks away.

I stopped the first person I met. "Do you know where I can find Jackie Goldman's office?"

The young woman gave me a quizzical look. "Are you that Joe Hammer guy everyone is talking about."

Oh man, I thought. "Yeah, that's me. Do you know where I can find Jackie Goldman?"

"Wow, I wouldn't want to be in your shoes for all the tea in China. Just so you know, I'd say that most of the people in this office think you are despicable. Fair warning, you not going to have a good day. Jackie's cubicle is in that corner," pointing over my left shoulder.

"Thank you."

"Hey, what can I say? Welcome to the team."

I made my way through the maze of cubicles. I noticed the messy cubicles with stacks of paper stashed in every available space toward the back of the bullpen area was Jackie Goldman's cubicle.

"Are you Jackie Goldman?" I asked, standing in the doorway to her cluttered cubicle.

By nodding yes and pointing to the headset she was wearing, she confirmed her identity. She pointed to the broken chair next to her desk. She turned her back to me and continued her conversation. I balanced myself on the broken chair and looked around her cubical. She turned around. "Hello Joe, it's been a long time since we crossed paths."

"I'm sorry for interrupting you. I didn't notice you were on the phone. Have we met before?"

"Well... kind of. I defended several people you were trying to lock up. I have to admit you were a formidable adversary. Oh well, such is life. Welcome to the public defender's office. Let's get a cup of coffee and find a room where we can talk in private."

The coffee pot was in a small, crowded supply room. It was also the only room where we could have a private conversation. While making a fresh pot of coffee, we chit-chatted about life and what it's like to be a lawyer. She retrieved two chairs, then began our conversation in the cramped quarters of the supply room.

My new boss Jackie sat in a chair and extended to arm to sit in the opposing chair. The friendly professional lawyer disappeared. Everything got serious. "It's hard to imagine what you've been through over the past couple of years. It takes a lot of courage to start. I want you to know that I want to be a positive influence on your new beginning. Let me tell you about the public defender's office. We have twenty-seven full-time lawyers, kids just out of law school. Some of these kids are true believers and other are the kids the big law firms passed on. The lawyers who work here handle an average of eighty open ongoing cases. That means we can't provide the defense that people deserve. Unfortunately, for economic reasons, we do a lot of plea deals. Seventy-five percent of our cases end with a plea bargain. It's not the best way of doing business, but under the circumstances, it's the best we can do. We have private practice lawyers that do pro bono cases, but we need a hundred more just to make a dent in our backlog. I can't bring myself to think about the innocent people who are sitting in prison because we lacked the money and the resources to build a good defense. That's about the extent of the public defender's office. Do you have questions or second thoughts?"

"No. I appreciate the opportunity."

Jackie looked away for a few seconds before turning in my direction. "Joe let's cut to the chase. To be successful in working in my office, the first thing you need to do is to cut the crap. I was Miguel Acosta's lawyer that advised him to take a plea deal. Your disdain for defense lawyers and the public defender's office is legendary. You don't want to be here anymore than I want you here. You are here out of necessity. I was glad to see you getting kicked out of the profession, goodbye and good riddance."

"I get it, I do."

"To be honest with you, I will treat you with kindness and respect. I expect nothing but the same from you toward me, the other lawyers, and to support people in this office. I'm a proud bleeding-heart liberal, which I consider being one of my best attributes. If you ever act out in this office the way you behaved in the DA's office, I will make sure you never work in this profession again. I promise you I'm the biggest, nastiest, maniacal bitch you'll ever meet. Don't even think of trying your bullshit on me or anyone else in this office. Are we on the same page?"

"I understand. The past two years have changed my life. In my meeting yesterday with Judge Horton, he made it clear how he felt about the way I've treated people over the years. I realize I had, and to a certain degree, still have a caustic personality. I promise you I'll do the best I can to be a productive member of your staff."

"Judge Horton put a lot of faith in you. He sees something the rest of us don't and I trust his judgement. Enough said Joe, let's move on. Let's talk about compensation. A new lawyer who's passed the bar starts in our office at forty thousand a year. They started out for three months under my supervision, handling around ten simple cases. The next three months, they take on more complex cases. After that, they do their business on their own. I watch them like a hawk. I give them more open cases to where it's almost too much. You don't need my supervision, but I want an update on the Jack Holt case. Since that's the only case the judicial review board will let you handle, your salary will be twenty-five thousand a year. I understand the wages are bad, but I have budget constraints," she said as she got up to get another cup of coffee. "Would you like a warmup?"

"No, thanks."

"I suspect this won't be much of a surprise. With the Jack Holt case, the prosecutor's office and the local media have already convicted your client. Joe, I want you to know that I believe with all my heart everyone deserves a second, third, and fourth chance. We should never give up on our fellow human beings. You need the opportunity to redeem yourself. And God knows I need all the help I can get. I promise I will be fair, open, honest and respectful of you. I know this has to be difficult for you. Nothing would make me happier than to see you make a successful comeback minus the shitty personality."

A soft knock on the supply room door interrupted their conversation.

"Come in, Eddy," Jackie said, facing the door. "I'd like to introduce Eduardo Rubio. He's the new lawyer who filled in for you on the Jack Holt case. His name is Eduardo, but everyone calls him Eddy. I asked him to make himself available this morning."

The door opened. A man who, at first appearance, looked too young to be a lawyer joined the conversation. Jackie tells him to find a chair in an empty cubicle. A few seconds later, he rolls a chair into the room.

"As Jackie sat down, she introduced the young lawyer. "Eddy, this is Joe Hammer."

I waited for Jackie to sit down before I could extend my hand. "Nice to meet you."

"Likewise. I don't know what you were expecting, but don't I have a lot of information about this case or this Jack Holt guy. I met him ten days ago. It was a few minutes before his arraignment for murder and sexual assault. When I told him I was from the public defender's office, he seemed unimpressed. They made the coroner's report on Maggie Stewart's autopsy public before the arraignment. The coroner concluded, based on the autopsy report, that her death was a homicide caused by strangulation. According to the report, she had sexual intercourse two hours before her death. The coroner speculated, based on his experience, it was two separate incidents. Jack Holt became a suspect when he refused to talk to the detectives without a lawyer. Within twenty minutes of meeting Mr. Holt, he was in custody. The next day, detectives got a search warrant to search his apartment. The warrant allowed the investigators to go through the entire house. In doing so, they got a toothbrush that had enough saliva to get a sample of Mr. Holt's DNA. The coroner's office ruled that the DNA found in Maggie Stewart's vagina and the DNA from the toothbrush was the same. The detectives then charged Jack Holt with first-degree sexual assault and first-degree murder."

"Did the detectives attempt to interrogate Mr. Holt even after he requested a lawyer?" I asked.

"Mr. Holt said nothing to that effect. What I know is the two detectives have been bugging the hell out of me to question him. Because of my schedule, I haven't had the time to consult with Mr. Holt and agree to a date and time. Yesterday they made another request, only this time they were planning to take it up the ladder. That's when Jackie told them you were taking over as Mr. Holt's lawyer. As of this moment, they're cooling their jets until you get up to speed. That's about all I can tell you about Jack Holt. He seems kind of distant and not willing to cooperate. I've only been a lawyer for a year. Most people I've defended are more than willing to cooperate and tell me right out they are innocent." With the folder in hand, he reached over and gave it to me.

"Do you have any idea why he's so aloof?" I asked.

"Maybe it's because I'm a rooky? I don't know. I asked him if he raped and murdered Maggie Stewart. He said no and nothing else. If I was innocent, and they accused me of crimes like this, I would be a hell of a lot more willing to cooperate with the lawyer representing me."

I opened the folder and scanned a few of his notes that repeated what he just heard. "Did you request the police report?"

"No, I haven't had the time. I have fifty active cases. I don't have the luxury of a small caseload. To me, he didn't come across like a guy that wanted a defense attorney. There are too many other cases where the accused want my help." He looked at Jackie. "What's so special about this guy? He gets a senior lawyer that's handling only one case. Is that fair? If I had to pick a guy to help, he'd be on the bottom of the stack."

Jackie looked at Joe, then turned to the junior lawyer. "Eddy, all I can say is I got a call from Judge Horton, who informed me that Joe would handle this case. He didn't bother to explain his reason. Did he say anything to you, Joe?"

"Not really. All Judge Horton said was that he had unfinished business and nothing else. He gave me his name and to come here today and start working on his defense."

"I just remembered something that might be important," said Eddy. "This Jack Holt guy's face is all messed up. I don't know for sure what caused it, but it's unavoidable. One guard in the county lockup said it looked to him like mix Bell's palsy and several hits from a big guy swinging a baseball bat. He also carries his body a little skewed to his left."

"How is that important to his situation?"

"It shouldn't be a factor at all, but I think it will be. All I can say for sure is you can't help but notice his face. It's a showstopper. Whether you want to admit it, it gets in the way. Do you remember that Super Bowl laundry detergent commercial a few years back?"

"I'm sorry?"

"In the commercial, there's this guy interviewing for a job. He has a stain on his shirt. It's a talking stain that consumes all the interviewer's attention. Jack Holt's face is kind of like that stain. It impeded our conversation. I know this doesn't sound good, but to be honest with you at first, the guy's facial features surprised me."

"Okay," I said, still not seeing any connection to his situation.

"I think that's about it. Do you have anything else you'd like to add?" asked Jackie.

"Nah, I wish I could help you more, but that's all I got," answered the junior lawyer.

"Thank you, Eddy," said Jackie.

"Let me know if I can help you out," said the junior lawyer as he took his chair and left the supply room.

"I wish we could have helped you out more on this case. Last week, Eddy put in eighty hours trying to help his clients. That's not unusual with my team. I discourage it because they burn themselves out, and that's not good for anyone. Joe, did the judge say why this guy is getting this special treatment?"

"No. I only spent thirty minutes with the judge. The fact is, I can't explain why I got such a break, much less this Jack Holt guy. My reputation leaves a lot to be desired. I will do my best to be an effective lawyer for my client and a productive team player on your team."

"There's one more thing. I don't have a cubicle ready for you until next week. If you see one that's empty, help yourself. Do you have a cell phone?"

"Yeah."

"You can use this supply room if you want, or you can work out of your house. Just remember, I want a verbal update. Also, if you run into a snag, let me know. Are we cool?"

"Yep."

"Good, I gotta run. Have fun."

• • • •

I sat for a few minutes, feeling like I'd been on a roller coaster. I realized this would be an uphill climb. Once again, having self-doubts. I found myself in the supply room, deep in thought about my next move. Should I just tell Jackie thanks but no thanks and move on? I wasn't sure I could take all the criticism, especially when every damn word of it was true.

"Hello," said a woman standing at the door, "are you okay?"

"I'm sorry I didn't hear you."

"I need to get some staples, but I didn't want to startle you."

"I apologize; I was daydreaming. I didn't even realize you were standing there. My name is Joe Hammer."

"I know who you are. My name is Hilda Gaspar," she answered as she smiled and shook hands. "I finally get to meet you. You're the talk of the office. I doubt you remember, but we worked at the DA's office just before you got disbarred. I was the intern who discovered that you'd railroaded an innocent man into prison. Just to be clear, I'm the one who ratted you out and cost you your job."

"You did the right thing by turning me in to the authorities. Thank you."

"Are you trying to be funny?"

"No, Hilda, I'm serious. I caused my demise. No one else. I did something wrong, and I paid the price for my indiscretion. I was lucky enough to get another opportunity. Most people aren't so fortunate. Please believe me, I was serious when I thanked you."

"I wanted you to know that I'm the person who reported you to Eric Warren. You were wrong to do what you did. You got what you deserved. I've since learned that sometimes justice is somewhere in between being right or wrong. Everyone deserves a second chance."

"It took me twenty years to come to that conclusion. I'm trying my best to make it work this time. Thanks to you, I also learned that lesson the hard way. Are you a lawyer?"

"I will be as soon as I pass the bar exam."

"Good for you. I wish you all the best. Thank you."

"For what?"

"For putting me in my place."

"I'd better get back to work."

For some strange reason, I felt better and a little like I was home.

Chapter 7

Henry Keller ~ Juror #3

My name is Henry Keller, the juror no one likes. Just before leaving my house for the courthouse this morning, my wife and I barely spoke. I'm not sure I know how to keep myself together. Sometimes I feel like I could explode.

My experience as a juror is so disappointing. "Our legal system is a mess from the way they picked our jury, through the trial, and especially now during the deliberations. A bitchy female judge makes a mousy woman foreperson. Unbelievable. If I were in charge, we'd be on our way home instead of voting."

It was time to vote and put this piece of human scum in prison for life. We can put this circus behind us and get on with our lives. I'm hoping we can move on.

"Sara?" said the foreperson with a pin in hand and waited for her response.

"Guilty."

Then she asked me, "How do you vote?"

"Guilty as hell," it was the easiest decision I'd made in years. My only regret is the legislature banned the death penalty. Those snowflake liberals are destroying this country.

"Marty?"

"Guilty."

"Mike?"

"Guilty."

"Linda?"

"Guilty."

"Kayla?"

"Guilty."

"Hassan?"

"Guilty."

"Alexandro?"

"Not guilty."

"Are you kidding me!" I said, looking at Alexandro. "There's always one. Why is there always someone who has to be weird?"

Linda shook her head in disgust at Alexandro's not-guilty vote.

"Please, we have a lot to do here. Keep your comments and your antics to yourselves. Let's keep going. Oscar?"

"Not guilty."

"Michael?"

"Guilty."

"I'm a guilty vote," said the foreperson.

Watching this spectacle, I could barely keep it together! I am pointing at the guy who casted the first innocent vote. "Why did you vote that way?"

"My name is Alexandro but call me Alex," responded Alex. "I would love to answer your question. First, I did not vote innocent. I voted not guilty and before you say anything, there's a big difference. I don't believe the prosecution proved their case against Mr. Holt."

"What are you talking about?" I asked.

"What I'm trying to say", answered Alex, "is I believe the DA's office used the local television stations to pander to the public's preconceived notions about certain people. Why is it when Marsh County Detention moved Mr. Holt to and from the prison the local media is right there? I also think it's a little odd that they always catch Mr. Holt in a prison orange jumpsuit and wearing shackles. Other inmates get to change before leaving the Marsh County Detention Center. It wouldn't surprise me if the prosecutor gave the local news people a heads up when they transferred him to and from the jail. Every night during the jury selection, the local stations aired something about this case. They've shown head shots of Mr. Holt and Mrs. Stewart. Make no mistake, the local media has tried and convicted Jack Holt. The prosecution is describing Maggie Stewart as a world class model worth millions. Through innuendo they sent the message that Mrs. Stewart would never have sexual intercourse with a man who looks like Mr. Holt."

The nonsense coming out of that guy's mouth was stunning. It was hard to listen to him. "Okay Poncho, you've got one muy grande imagination."

"Henry, that's it," said the foreperson. She stood up from her chair, looking at me. "I'm taking your insulting racist remarks to the judge. Your comments are disgusting. There's no room for that behavior on this jury." She got up, went to talk to the bailiffs.

"Okay," I said, "I was out of line. It won't happen again, I promise." I couldn't help but wonder when we started having to always be so damn correct? I watched the foreperson, and the bailiff talk in muffled voices. The bailiff signaled her to come outside as he shut the door to the jury room. The jury was speculating about what would happen next. After taking a deep breath, I stood up, and I walked to the window. I watched the rain clouds move across the afternoon sky.

· · · ·

It had only been two months since I'd been home. After returning, my wife and my youngest son, Gary, seemed on edge. I figured it was because they weren't used to having me around.

The day before I reported for jury duty, our oldest son, Hank, came home from college for the weekend. Everything seemed fine until we sat down for dinner. My wife and sons seemed anxious. I'm a cut through bullshit kind of person. "Okay, is there something going on that I need to know?" My sons looked at my wife.

"Henry," my wife put her hand on my arm, "you have to promise you won't come unglued."

"No, I won't promise that. Just tell me what the hell is going on."

Hank sitting across from me looked at me. "While you were in Iraq, I came out to mom and Gary. They're worried about how you're going to react to me being gay."

Since he was a boy, it was important to me to instill in him what it meant to be a real man. Now I'm finding it difficult to even look at that faggot. My wife and sons weren't sure how I'd take the news. I get up from the table and walked out of the dining room.

"I'm sorry, dad."

What he said was hard to believe. "Did you say you were sorry?" Looking at him with nothing but contempt. Grabbing him by his shirt and dragging him to the front door with every intent to throw him out and disown him. "You're dead!"

Hank seemed resigned to my expected reaction. He didn't show the slightest sign of fear. He told me to get my hands off him, then pushed me away.

Gary, my other son, got between Hank and me. "Move," I said.

"No," Gary answered.

"Henry, if you don't calm down, I'll call the police," said my wife who stood behind me.

"Dad, I'll leave. Please don't do this to Mom and Gary," Hank said as he left the house.

My parting words as he left our house, "Get out, you're dead!"

"What the hell is wrong with you?" asked my wife. "Why did you humiliate your own son? You don't know when to shut up. Henry, he idolizes you."

"Get him out of my sight. Do you understand what I'm saying? Quit trying to get me to apologize. You're wasting your time. He's dead, end of the subject."

"Dad, we're tired of you talking to us like we report to you," Gary responded.

"Henry, you will be on that jury for a while. When you get back, you'd better make it right between you and Hank. We're tired of your nonstop toxic masculinity. You need to suck it up and clean up the mess you made with your sons. Then you need to get counseling. Henry, you need to take care of these issues. If you don't, we're done."

• • • •

The opening door interrupted my thoughts. It had been ten minutes since the foreperson had gone to talk to the judge. The silence among the other jurors was deafening. Everyone was on edge. I could hear only muffled whispers between people. Most likely complaining about me being a loudmouth jackass.

"Could I please have everyone's attention?" said the foreperson as she stood behind her chair at the head of the table. "I had a conversation with our bailiff, Gus. He wants to talk to everyone." The foreperson took her seat.

"I won't waste time," said the bailiff. "Judge Taylor has mentioned several times she expects jurors to take their responsibilities serious. Let's get something straight right up front. Mrs. Fischer did not ask to be the foreperson. The judge did not give her an option. That's it. There was no ulterior motive. I recommended I talk to you before we escalate this situation to Judge Taylor. A complaint this early in deliberations would not go over well with the Judge. Believe it or not, I'm doing you a favor. Mrs. Fischer did not mention any names during our conversation, so I don't know who is making racist remarks. I can tell you if this happens again, there will be severe consequences. It could mean felony criminal charges and serious time behind bars. Here's what it comes down to. Take your responsibilities as jurors serious. I can assure you the lawyers do, Judge Taylor does, as does the entire legal system of the United States. Just do your duty." Gus left the jury room.

"I apologize. It's difficult to understand why you people can't see what's going on here. I've never seen a more guilty man in my life. My only regret is our liberal legislature did away with the death penalty. I'd love to see Holt get what he deserves, the needle."

"Henry," said Alex. "Like I said, I'm not saying he's innocent. I just don't think the prosecution has much of a case, and they didn't prove beyond a reasonable doubt that he's guilty."

The foreperson, still frustrated, tells everyone to take a break to get some refreshments.

Ten minutes later...

"Let's get back to work," said the foreperson. The break didn't dispel the frustration after the first vote. The jury had to be told again to take their seats.

Linda, becoming frustrated, stood up and addressed her fellow jurors. "Sit your asses down in your chair, now!"

Kayla Rooney, sitting next to Linda, said, "Girl, you need to chill. When was the last time you got laid?"

Linda looks at Kayla. "You'd be smart to shut your mouth."

"You've got a serious attitude for being such a scrawny white girl," Kayla whispered. "Whatever you do, just watch your mouth around me."

The foreperson doesn't understand why Linda and I have been trying to get things done.

"When I was in the army, I had ways of getting everyone's undivided attention," I told the foreperson. "Your jury is out of control. Are you going to do something or what?"

"Linda and Henry," said the foreperson. "If you don't like me being the foreperson, then take it to Gus. I'll be happy to get him in here if you'd like. Until then, I suggest we talk about the case?"

"Speaking for myself and not Johnny America down there," Linda said, referring to me. "I suggest that since the vote was ten to two, I think those who voted not guilty should explain how they came to that ridiculous conclusion. Maybe the rest of us could help you understand the evidence. How about if one of you could share with us why you voted the way you did?"

The foreperson shook her head in disbelief.

"I'd be happy to explain why I voted not guilty," responded Alex. "I can only speak for myself. You'll have to ask Mr. Rosenthal why he voted not guilty. The reason I voted not guilty means the prosecution didn't prove Mr. Holt's guilt beyond a reasonable doubt. When the autopsy report came out, it identified Mr. Holt's semen in Maggie Stewart. On that fact alone, the prosecution concluded that Mr. Holt sexually assaulted her. Neither the police nor the prosecutor bothered reading the entire autopsy report. As soon as the coroner's report came out, detectives focused on proving Jack Holt's guilt. I'm not a woman, nor have I ever been sexually molested. A woman would at least try to protect herself from the rapist. She would use everything possible to protect herself. The most obvious way would be her fingernails. It's a little odd that right there in the coroner's report it says they found nothing under Mrs. Stewart's fingernails."

"That's not odd at all," said Ira McMillian. "If the rapist overwhelmed her by force, she wouldn't have thought about using her fingernails."

"It makes perfect sense," said Linda Sawyer. "Just because they found nothing doesn't mean Jack Holt didn't rape her."

"What?" said Kayla Rooney. "that's a load. If some dude tried to rape me, there'd be a lot of him under my fingernails. That dude would be have'n some major pain. Foreperson, would you change my vote to innocent?"

"What? If we keep talking about all these pie in the sky theories, we'll get nothing accomplished," I said, leaning back in my chair.

"We are in pursuit of justice. You can draw your own conclusions," answered Alex. "I think the fact there was no DNA under Mrs. Stewart's fingernails is odd. According to the coroner's report, there were no signs of violence found anywhere on Maggie Stewart's body other than her neck where the murderer strangled her."

"Whatever?" said Linda Sawyer.

"What about her husband?" asked Alex. "When he was on the stand, there was something about him that made me wonder. Did anyone else have that feeling? The prosecution based their entire case on the assumption Mrs. Stewart would never have intercourse with a man who looks like Mr. Holt. Something bothers me about the way the prosecution handled this case. I think they were lazy."

"If I were the prosecutor, that's how I would have presented the evidence against the man that raped her," said Ira McMillian. "In reality, a wealthy and beautiful woman like Mrs. Stewart would never have sexual intercourse with a guy who looks like Jack Holt. I know some of you want to believe that it could happen. In reality, it would never happen under any circumstances. Those two people did not have consensual intercourse. Never in a million years would that happen! Not only that, but the defense lawyer claimed that Maggie Stewart and Jack Holt had a romantic relationship. Everyone in this room knows damn good and well that assertion is nothing but a pipe dream."

"Is that right? Sounds to me like you have it all figured out. How can you make such a statement?" asked Kayla Rooney, sitting at the end of the table opposite the foreperson. "My husband and I got married twenty-four years ago. As you can see, I'm a tall, stout, black woman and my husband is a damn good look'n well hung white dude. When we go out in public, people look at us like we're a black and white version of Mutt and Jeff. Hell, I'm eight inches taller than him. When I was growing up, I knew without a doubt I'd marry a handsome black man. I believed that until I met my husband, then my world changed. I not only think it's possible, but I also think it is likely Jack and Maggie had been a couple."

"Oh, come on," said Linda. "That's easy for you to say. In reality, there's no way you or me would have a romantic relationship with Jack Holt. There was no possibility of a relationship between them, it never happened. Nothing ever happened other than him stocking her, raping her, and then murdering her. It's that simple. Let's not make this case more difficult than it is."

"What about the evidence and testimony that says otherwise?" asked Kayla.

"That so-called evidence is baloney," Linda answered, staring at Kayla. "Fabricated by that weasel of a defense attorney."

Kayla looked at Linda. "Like when you told everyone your blouse cost four-hundred bucks?"

"There's no point in trying to reason with you people."

"You people?" questioned Kayla. "What's that supposed to mean?"

"Yeah," said Mike Shepard, a black man sitting on the other side of Linda. "I'd love to hear your answer."

"I'll tell you something," said Linda. "I want to get the hell out of here. We should focus on the issues only. Some of you bleeding hearts are causing the fighting between us with your crazy ideas."

"Well, I'm sorry the deliberation is such a bother for you. I have to tell you the vote is now nine to three," said Kayla. "You weren't listening. I already told everyone that I changed my mind. Just talking to you made me rethink why I voted guilty."

I can't believe our foreperson doesn't take charge of the situation. I don't understand why the judge would choose such a weak person to be the foreperson. Maybe I should, for the sake of the entire jury, go to the judge.

"All right," said the foreperson. "That's enough. Oscar, is there anything you'd like to say?"

"Dr. Molina could have spoken to me. I agree with everything he said. The prosecution did not prove guilt beyond a reasonable doubt."

"Okay, stop," I said. "The defense didn't prove him innocent."

The foreperson sat up in her chair. "Are you serious, Henry? The defense doesn't need to prove him innocent. In our justice system, the role of the defense attorney is to disprove the prosecution's case against their client. He's innocent until proven guilty beyond a reasonable doubt. The prosecution's entire case against Mr. Holt is circumstantial, not to mention somewhat bigoted. I'm not an expert in criminal law, but to be honest with you, the police and the prosecution didn't do their job. They are prosecuting Mr. Holt for the way he looks, and they are playing on our prejudices to get an easy conviction. Mr. Holt is easy. I realize it's hard to believe, but that's what I think they're doing."

"I apologize for interrupting you," said Marty Chu. "Do you think a prosecutor would stoop that low to get a conviction? Hard to believe. The prosecution had a witness who testified that Mr. Holt is a pathological liar. Other witnesses testify he had trouble holding a job. Police arrested him two times for drunk driving and police have taken him to jail on suspicion of domestic violence."

"The prosecution proved without question that Jack Holt is a person with a troubled past," said Oscar. "I'm not arguing that point. All those people made their case against him. If you remember during jury selection when the prosecution asked each of us if we had issues with Mr. Holt's facial features? That seemed to me to be an odd question to ask someone. To me, it was a ploy to downplay a logical assumption about Mr. Holt's facial disfigurement. Understand, I want to be fair to everyone in this situation. Someone murdered and buried Mrs. Stewart in a park. I don't want to rush to judgment because it's easy to do. I'd vote guilty if the prosecution proved his guilt beyond a reasonable doubt. The fact is they didn't."

"You must admit," said Michael Eckert, sitting to the right of the foreperson, "the likelihood of Mr. Holt having consensual sex with a world-famous model would never happen in a million years."

"That's my entire point," answered Dr. Alejandro Molina. "That we are discussing this man's facial features is at the heart of this case. The fact is, we don't know for sure that Mrs. Stewart did or didn't have a romantic relationship with Mr. Holt. The fact is that we as a society put a high value on how things look, especially people. As a society, we have come to where everything has to look perfect. We surround ourselves with good-looking people who live in perfect looking neighborhoods. We watch television and the movies where everyone is a perfect specimen of what an ideal human should look like. Unfortunately, the evil guys are dependable exceptions. Actors play the villain using make up to disfigure their face. I've always had crooked teeth when I was a child in the forties and fifties. No one gave my teeth a second thought. My grandson inherited my crooked teeth. My daughter has spent thousands getting his teeth straightened to make him easy on the eye. I'm not an expert on this subject, but our priorities are not what they should be."

"Dr. Molina, I understand your point, but I'm afraid I don't agree with it," responded Michael Eckert. "I don't judge people by the color of their skin, their ethnicity, or their appearance."

"Mr. Eckert," said Dr. Molina. "May I ask you something?"

"Sure."

"You stated you don't judge people by the color of their skin, their ethnicity, or how they look. Did I understand you correctly?"

"Yes."

"Do you think other people discriminate against others based on color, ethnicity, weight, or Mr. Holt's facial appearance?"

Michael Eckert looked at Dr. Molina. "I'm not sure how to answer your question."

"There's no right or wrong way to answer. How do you feel?"

"Yeah, I feel there are people bigoted toward minorities, ethnic groups, and yeah, I guess their facial features too."

"So, if I'm correct, you believe we as a country still judge people by skin color, ethnicity and to some extent their facial features? The country feels that way, but you don't. Is that correct?"

"Ah, come on. What's all this have to do with the guy who's on trial?" I said, doing everything possible not to explode. "Earlier, Rosenthal called you a doctor. What kind of doctor are you? Are you some kind of expert?"

"Henry, based on what you've said, that you're a military man," responded Oscar Rosenthal. "I have nothing but respect for those who put their lives on the line for our country. I mean that, thank you. Sir, you have an impolite way of referring to people that sometimes doesn't sit well with others, me included."

I stood up and walked to the window. I couldn't help but think these people would acquit this guy. As sure as the sun will rise tomorrow morning, he will stalk and kill another innocent woman. I was having a hard time even looking at these people. Without turning around, I told them, "I'm not in any hurry. I can be here for the next month. If we ever hope to decide, we need to stop getting off track. This is a ridiculous waste of everyone's time and has nothing to do with this man's guilt."

Chapter 8

Jack Holt

"So?"

"Hey Leto," I answered. "So? What do you mean?"

"How did your day go at the courthouse?"

"The prosecution is mentioning every stupid thing I ever did in my entire life."

"That's not so good, amigo. Did that brown sugar help you get some sleep?"

"I know it's dangerous, but I slept like a baby and had the best dreams."

"I'm glad it worked out for you. Just be careful you don't want to become a junkie."

"Yeah, I hear you. You think it's possible that I can get worse off than I already am? My lawyer thinks I will get off. I think he's pumping sunshine."

"How is your lawyer doing when he cross examines people who testify against you?"

"Ugh, most of the people on the stand today had nothing but crappy things to say about me. They took the stand to tell the jury how much of a creep I am. My lawyer tried his best, but what they said was true. The thing is everything they said today had nothing to do with Maggie's death. Her doctor husband testified. He's one weird dude. I hope the jury saw how strange he was."

"You're innocent, right?"

"Who's asking you or the prosecutor who asked you to spy on me? Never mind, it doesn't matter the answer's the same. I had nothing to do with Maggie's murder. Her loony ass doctor husband killed her, but we can't prove it. Damn, I hope things will change when my lawyer tells my side. Leto, are you telling the prosecution everything we talk about?"

"Hell no, I'm not a puto snitch. Believe me, amigo, I haven't said a word to anyone about you. I swear to Our Lady of Guadalupe. Not to mention I'm not that stupid. I'm in here for selling drugs if that's not bad enough all I need is for you to rat me out for supplying you brown sugar heroin."

"Oh yeah, that's a good point. I won't sell you out! Okay Leto, I'm tired. I'm hitting the sack. Good night." I put half of a brown sugar pill on my tongue and swallowed it with a big drink of water.

"Good night, bro."

The comforting warmth of the drug running through my body; I was free.

· · · ·

"Look what the cat drug in. It's Mr. Jack," said Maggie as she stood at the counter talking to Reggie Hardaway, the owner of Reggie's Coffee Shop. "I've been looking for you, big boy. Can I buy you a cup of coffee?"

"Hey Jack," Reggie said to me as he turned around. "Thanks for including me in your dream."

"If you dream about drinking coffee, will that keep you awake?" I asked.

"Good question, I don't know, but I will make you a small latte with one sugar."

"You don't have to buy," I said to Maggie. "I don't know you yet."

"We talked about this before you're dreaming. This is where I return the towels and discover Reggie's coffee shop by the park, the best kept secret in the city. Is there any way possible I can get a big smooch and hug? That would make my day."

We embraced and gave each other a kiss.

"Come on, guys, knock it off. You're acting like kids. Go get a room," said Reggie as he gave Maggie her coffee. "Since this is a dream, the coffee is on the house." Reggie turns to me. "Yours is coming right up."

"Remember, we don't know each other yet. You're captivated by my stunning beauty and effervescent personality," said Maggie with her alluring grin. "Would you like to sit down and talk?"

"Sure, can I ask you something?"

"You can ask me anything."

"What were you thinking when you came here to return the towels? The towels weren't worth much."

"I wanted to meet you. You were so sweet when we first met that morning in the park. I had to have a reason to meet you, and I had three bar towels."

"Why don't you two grab a table and I'll bring your drink out to you," Reggie suggested.

"Sounds good, Reggie," answered Maggie.

Maggie had me enthralled. I said to her as we walked to a table in the corner next to Rosemont Street. "Meeting you changed my life for the better."

"Mr. Jack. This is a dream, and I know everything you know because of that. That somehow, I changed you for the better. We met each other and because we met, we both changed for the better. I'm crazy in love with you. I'm broken on the inside like you're broken on the outside."

"Here's your latte, Jack," said Reggie.

Maggie leans in close to Jack and whispers, "Did you notice how that old man in the corner eyeballs all the women?"

"What guy?" I answered as I turned around to see who she was talking about.

"Don't do that," Maggie whispered. "If his eyes were laser beams, they would blow my ass to smithereens. He's harmless, but he's still a little creepy."

"He's been staring at my ass," I said, attempting to be funny.

"Not to worry, Mr. Jack, I still love you even though you're flawed. I want to be serious with you for a minute. You look tired. How are you holding up? Is the trial becoming too much?"

"Yeah, the prosecution is bringing up all the things I've hidden in the closet. They're going after my credibility, and I think it's working. It's difficult listening to all the dumbass things I've done."

"Is your lawyer doing his job?"

"Yeah, I think so, but what the hell do I know? Can't be too critical of him. He's my only option. A trial is a crapshoot for anybody. Even though my lawyer tells me not to look at the jury now and then, I glance in their direction. They make me wonder, how many of them pegged me as guilty the instant they laid eyes on me?"

"I'm sorry, Jack. If I could make all this go away for you, I would. It breaks my heart you're on trial. It makes me want to scream as loud as I can."

"My lawyer believes I'm innocent. He met with Penelope Bergdorf; he changed his mind. I told him about your plans to divorce your husband. He wanted to know your lawyer's name. At first, all I could remember was she had a reputation for being a fierce lawyer. Then, out of the blue, he asked me if it was Penelope Bergdorf. It blew me away that he picked that lawyer's name! How did he do that? It turns out he went through a divorce, and she was his wife's lawyer. He wasn't at all thrilled to meet with her. The irony of his reluctance to have a meeting with her was that he came back with a better strategy in defending me. He never told me what went on during his meeting, but from my point of view, it was positive."

"Penelope told me her investigator uncovered that my husband and some bigwig in the DA's office were into some creepy sex stuff," said Maggie. "There's a sex club in town that both were charter members. I don't know why that would get your lawyer worked up or if it's something else? All I want it to do is to get you off. If only I could do something other than visit you in your dreams."

•   •   •   •

Sunday mornings at Reggie's were like a special occasion held every Sunday morning. Reggie and his sister go all out with gourmet pastries, breakfast burritos, and other good eats. The offering on the menu at Reggie's Coffee Shop for the Sunday brunch special was incredible.

The regular Sunday morning crowd was doing its thing. After I got my latte, the Sunday paper, and a breakfast burrito, I looked around for a table. I remember the first time I noticed her as she stood up and waved at me.

"If you join me, I would love to visit with you," she said with her incredible smile.

"Sorry, I didn't see you when I walked in." She terrified me. What would she want with me? What is she trying to prove? Is she one of those bleeding-heart types that want to treat me like her pet? I'm not sure I trust her. Besides, I couldn't remember her name. "Are you sure?"

"I'm positive," she answered. "I'll even help you eat your burrito."

"If you insist," I responded as I sat down across from her. I still could not remember her name. Lane, Laura, Lauren, Lindsay. What the hell was her name? "How have you been?"

"I'm fine, Jack. How are you?"

'Oh man,' I thought, 'How did she remember my name and I couldn't remember hers?' "I'm doing great. What a surprise to see you! What are you making?"

"A friendship bracelet. It's great to see you here. I just love this little place."

"It's beautiful. What are you making those bracelets with?"

"I'm using different colored parachute cords."

"It looks great."

"It's a carryover from my girl scout days up in Sacramento. I find it relaxing. Do you want one?"

"Sure, I'll take one."

She reached into her purse and pulled out a handful. "Take your pick."

"Oh wow. I'll take the green and yellow one."

"Ah ha, you have excellent taste Jack," said Maggie. "Here you need a couple more. They'll spice up your life." She smiled. "What have you been up to?"

"Not much. I get up, go to work, go home, read a little and sometimes I watch a little TV. Then I do it all over again. I grab a bite here at Reggie's in the morning. That's the highlight of my day."

"Reggie told me you work down the street from here."

"Yeah, that's right. I work at BPL contract manufacturing. They stuff circuit boards with electronic components. I work in the warehouse with two other guys. We ship the finished product to wherever our customer is. How about you? What do you do?"

"I'm a homemaker. My husband is a gastroenterologist."

"What kind of..."

"He looks up people's rear ends with a camera to see if they're okay."

"What a way to make a living. I think I'd rather be a dentist."

"Me too! At least he doesn't come home and talk about all the stuff that's going on in the office."

Out of nowhere, a cute girl approached their table. "Are you Maggie Navarro?"

"Yes, I am. And who are you?"

"My name is Ava Rose Miller."

"How are you this morning, Miss Ava?"

"I'm fine. I'm so excited. Is there any way possible I can get your autograph and a picture of you with me, my brother, and my cousins?"

"You can," answered Maggie. "How old are you, Ava?"

"I'm nine years old. Could you please wait here while I get a piece of paper?" She hurried back to the table where her parents, her aunt, and uncle are sitting with her little brother and three cousins.

"So, you're famous?" I asked.

"No. When I was young, I was a model, so some girls know me that way," answered Maggie.

"I can see where you'd be a model. You're attractive."

"Thank you. I'm not a model anymore. They said I got too fat."

"No kidding? You don't appear to be a person who has a weight issue."

"I don't have a weight issue. The people who wanted to photograph me said I had a weight problem. I told them they had an ex-model problem, so I quit."

"Good for you. I guess? Right?"

"Hello," said the girl, holding an index card, a pin, and her mother's iPhone. "This is my little brother Luke, and these are my cousins, Brenden, Isabella, and Caroline. Do you mind taking a photo with us?"

"Not at all," answered Maggie as she pointed in my direction. "How about having my friend Jack snap a few shots?"

"Nice to meet you," I said.

"Do you mind?" said Ava, handing the camera to me.

"My pleasure," I answered, taking the smartphone.

"Do you know how to use it?"

"I sure do," I answered as I took two photos of the beautiful children and Maggie. Afterwards, the youngest child, a cute girl named Caroline, looked at me and said, "Did you know you look like my Papa?"

"I didn't know that" I answered. "He must be a handsome man?"

"He is."

"Can I give you something?" said Maggie as she reached into her purse. "Would you like a friendship bracelet?"

"Sure."

"Here's nine of them for everyone in your family," said Maggie.

"Thank you."

"You're very welcome."

With a bundle of friendship bracelets in hand, she ran back to their table.

"What were we talking about?" asked Maggie.

"You were talking about quitting your modeling job."

"Oh yeah, that's right. I'll find another job. Hell, I might even work for Reggie."

"There you go. You could even walk to work like me," I said as I cut my breakfast burrito in half. "Would you like half of my burrito?"

"Heck yeah. I'm hungry and that looks amazing," Maggie answered.

"Are you from here?" I asked.

"No, I was born in Los Angeles and raised in Sacramento. I have two older siblings, David and Elaina. Where are you from?"

"I was also born in Los Angeles. I moved here when I first met my ex-wife. We got divorced fourteen years ago. She and my son now live up in Portland, Oregon."

"That's too bad, but we all have our share of baggage," answered Maggie with her mouth full of food. "This burrito is delicious. So, what do you do in your spare time?"

"Like I said, I'm a bore, to be honest with you. I get home from work, make a sandwich, and read that's about it. How about you?"

"I have to admit, I'm a bit of a bore myself. The older I get, the more I like just hanging out. I enjoy reading novels, suspense stories."

"I imagined you being a former model, being part of the jet set crowd."

"Oh yeah? Well, you'd be wrong," answered Maggie.

"Did you enjoy being a model?"

"When you're young, it's a glamorous life. Models are beautiful girls. They fly around the globe wearing amazing clothes. They hang out on the French Riviera, in New York, or wherever a child thinks glamorous people hang out." Maggie takes a sip of her coffee. "It's not that way at all. I was seventeen when my mother and I ran into an agent at a mall in Sacramento. The first thing they did was to change my name from Norma to Maggie. I did some modeling around Sacramento, then I got a job in Chicago where I met my agent from New York. That's when my career took off. In reality, I was just a hunk of skinny meat that clothes designers hung their wares on. I weighed ninety pounds. My agent suggested I smoke to suppress my appetite. It didn't take long for me to be smoking two packs a day. I was a successful model, but to be honest, I had nothing to do with it. My mom and dad have to take the credit, they made me. All the photographers and my agent cared about were my tits and ass. I was making more money than I ever imagined. As long as I got the big paychecks, I was fine. Take all the pics of my ass and tits you want."

"I can't even imagine. Congratulations on being so successful, that's great."

"Oh yeah, I suppose. It's a hard business for every successful model. There are thousands that aren't. They treat even the successful girls bad. We are nothing more than a slab of meat."

Our second meeting was much more relaxing than our first. Until Reggie's sister told us they were closing, we sat at the small table and talked. We told each other how we had enjoyed the good food and the conversation. We didn't make plans to see each other again but wished each other well. After an uncomfortable hug, we went our separate ways.

Chapter 9

Joe Hammer

Recovering from my nasty divorce and in need of an inkling of comfort, I purchased a used vintage fifties chrome and Formica-topped dinette set at a garage sale. It reminded me of my mom's kitchen. The dinette set became the centerpiece of my small studio apartment and made it almost bearable. I would sit at my dinette set for hours contemplating my future, or lack thereof.

My first day as a lawyer for the public defender's office was exhausting. No one I interacted with held back their low opinion of me. They shared how much of a son of a bitch I was and how they dreaded working with me. When I arrived back at my apartment, I had little energy to move. I struggled to get enough strength to open a bottle of water and relax at my dinette set. I sat staring into my empty apartment for at least an hour, immersed in self-pity and reflecting on what a depressing day it had been. Being able to practice law again came at an enormous emotional price. It was hard to accept that most of the people who either worked for me, with me, or just knew me hated me. Judge Horton gave me another chance to practice law. I haven't been able to sleep since. It was so bad that I had bags under my flushed, bloodshot eyes. I looked and felt like I had a terrible hangover. This time, I added a shot of Maker's Mark to another bottle of water that I opened. I took a deep breath and, little by little, I came to life. After three calls to the information systems helpline, I could download the police and autopsy reports that Jackson Maynard had mentioned. I shrugged off my feelings of despair. I decided I'd work through this period in my life.

As I read the police report, I remembered the junior lawyer at the public defender's office mentioning how disturbing Jack Holt's facial features were. The police report omitted how his face had become disfigured. I studied his mug shot on the police report for a long time. His childhood auto accident contorted the tissue around his left eye. His left eye looked like the accident burned it. The cheekbone that would define the left side of his face was missing. His jaw sank in on the left, causing his facial features to appear triangular. The left side of his face had a significant droop to it, starting from his forehead down to his neck. It looked as if it was just hanging. It was difficult to get a clear idea of his facial features because of the poor quality of the mug shot. There appeared to be a deep crevice that ran across his face, from his nose to his left ear, his head tilted to the left. I spent a considerable amount of time studying his facial features. I read the day-by-day, hour-by-hour account of the detectives' investigation.

Saturday morning-9:18AM:

Detectives Jerry Nichols and Russell Templeton went to Homestead Park. A Girl Scout troop doing a community service project uncovered human remains. The scoutmaster called 911. When Nichols and Templeton arrived, the CSI team was already exhuming the unidentified corpse. The park police had blocked off the scene with yellow crime scene tape.

Saturday afternoon-time not recorded.

The detectives talked to Homestead Park rangers and maintenance people. They learned workers prepared the soil three weeks before to make room for a community vegetable garden. The maintenance people added fertilizer and nutrients before turning the soil two feet deep. They completed the job eight days before. Someone buried the body in the soil after the park's maintenance people had turned the soil.

Monday afternoon–time not recorded.

Notes from autopsy: The coroner identified the body of Maggie Navarro Stewart. Her husband, Dr. Daniel Stewart, MD, reported her missing five days earlier. The autopsy report noted that her death was a homicide by strangulation. The coroner noted that two opposing thumb marks crushed her airway, causing her death. Another notable finding was the fact that she had had sexual intercourse as early as two hours before her death. The coroner noted in the report that there were no signs of injuries or evidence associated with sexual assault.

Detectives were unsuccessful in contacting Dr. Daniel Stewart. There was no answer on their home phone or at his office. Their intent was to inform him that the authorities had identified the remains of his wife in the park near their home.

Tuesday morning:

Detective Nichols contacted Dr. Stewart and requested a meeting at his home. The detectives inform the doctor that the coroner identified his wife's remains buried in the park behind their house. Whoever murdered Mrs. Stewart buried her less than a hundred feet from her backyard.

The detectives interviewed the doctor at his home for ninety minutes. They noted the doctor's cool and collected response to his wife's death as unusual. The doctor suggested the detectives talk to the neighbor; a woman named Marilyn Pope. He said she had seen a man around their home on the morning of the day Maggie disappeared.

The detectives interview Marilyn Pope. Both detectives noted in the report that she said in quotation marks. "She saw a creepy-looking man lurking around the Stewart's home on the morning of the day Maggie disappeared." When asked to further explain what she meant, she couldn't explain his features other than saying he was creepy looking. Detective Templeton pushed Mrs. Pope to give more details of the man's facial appearance, but she couldn't. Templeton noted that Mrs. Pope said it was difficult to look at him.

Tuesday afternoon:

It was after four o'clock on Tuesday afternoon when Detectives Nichols and Templeton arrived at the scene where they discovered Maggie Stewart's body. Detective Templeton was taking photographs of the crime scene when he noticed a man walking north on the park's main trail. The man, according to his notes in the police report, fit the description that Marilyn Pope described. Detective Templeton focused his camera on the man as he walked through the park. He asked Detective Nichols to yell as loud as he could. When Nichols yelled, the man turned in his direction. Detective Templeton took several photographs with his digital camera. The man looked a little surprised, went back to walking on the path. As they watched him walking north on the main trail, he stopped to rest on a park bench for a few minutes. Detective Nichols followed the man. Detective Templeton took the car to the north entrance of the park and waited for the man to appear.

They tag team the man as he made his way to the Quail Run apartment complex near the north entrance of the park. He entered apartment 215H-Building H. The detectives noted the man lived less than a mile northwest from the victim's home on Briarwood Lane in the Chapel Creek gated community. His apartment is also situated less than a mile from where Mrs. Stewart's body was found. The detectives go to the office, show their badges, and ask who lives in apartment 215H. The nervous clerk gave them Jack Holt's name.

Marilyn Pope confirmed the identity of the man in the photographs as the person at the Stewart's house the day she disappeared. The detectives return to the Quail Run Apartments to talk to Jack Holt. When they knocked on his apartment door, no one answered. They wait for about an hour before deciding to return early the next morning.

Wednesday morning 6:30AM

On a hunch, Detectives Nichols and Templeton wait in the parking lot near his apartment to follow him. At 6:45AM Jack Holt, a person of interest, leaves his apartment and walks south through the park on the main trail. Detective Nichols takes the car and drives to the south entrance across the street from Reggie's Coffee Shop by the Park. He parks the car and waits for his partner. Detective Templeton follows Mr. Holt on foot as he makes his way through the park, going toward the south entrance. To avoid suspicion, when Nichols sees him at the entrance, Templeton stops following.

Wednesday morning 7:03AM

Jack Holt crosses Red Oak Grove Boulevard after exiting the south entrance of Homestead Park. He goes to Reggie's Coffee Shop, buys a morning paper, orders a cup of coffee, and reads the paper. The detectives wait across the street, watching the entrance to the coffee shop.

Wednesday morning 7:49AM

Mr. Holt comes out of the coffee shop and waits for the signal at the intersection of Red Oak Grove Boulevard and Broadway Road. When the light changed, he crossed the street and walked south for two blocks.

Wednesday morning 7:56AM

Jack Holt enters the front door of BPL Contract Manufacturing. Detective Nichols watched the front entrance. Detective Templeton goes to the back to make sure the man doesn't leave. As Detective Templeton watches the loading dock, he sees Mr. Holt using a forklift to take boxes into the building. After an hour of watching, the detectives conclude that Jack Holt works at BPL Contract Manufacturing.

Wednesday morning 9:15AM

The detectives go back to Reggie's Coffee Shop to have a cup of coffee. While at the coffee shop, they make up a story about a facial disfigured man who lost his cell phone on a trail in the park. The older black man, Reggie Hardaway, who owned it, recognized it as Jack Holt's phone and provided the detectives with Jack's name. He also told him where Jack Holt worked and showed them the building just two blocks south on Broadway.

Wednesday morning 9:55AM

The detectives do more research on Jack Holt to see if he has a criminal record before they investigate further. Detective Nichols investigates Dr. Daniel Stewart's history while his partner investigates Jack Holt's history. Detective Templeton notes that there are only two people of interest: Dr. Daniel Stewart and Jack Holt. A star shows their primary interest is Dr. Stewart, not Jack Holt.

Joe notices in the police file that some numbered pages are missing. Page one has the name of Dr. Daniel Stewart along with his address, contact numbers, and email address. Detective Nichols made a note that Dr. Stewart had been working at the time his wife had disappeared. Nichols also noted that he thought it unusual that the doctor would know when his wife disappeared. Joe then notices there appears to be three pages missing from Dr. Stewart's suspect profile. Mr. Holt, as a person of interest profile, begins on page five.

Jack Holt's profile is intact. It showed he lives at the Quail Run Apartments, Building H, in apartment 215H. The detective verified Jack Holt's photograph they had taken against mug shots that were on file. Two women accused Jack Holt of unwanted and inappropriate sexual advances on two separate occasions. In both cases, the women dropped their complaints without reason. Mr. Holt had two DUI charges. In both cases, he pleads guilty. On his first offense, he had to attend alcohol awareness counseling for six months. The court fined him two thousand dollars for his second offense and suspended his driver's license for a year. It also required mandatory alcohol awareness meetings. The police took him into custody for domestic violence, but they didn't file any charges against him. Both offenses happened eleven years before.

Wednesday afternoon 2:35PM:

The captain summoned the detectives to his office. They noted that the district attorney himself had called to find out why they were looking into Dr. Daniel Stewart...

I thought it was odd that the rest of the notes made by the detectives were missing. I looked around the twenty-three-page file to see if I had missed this section. Something wasn't right about the police report.

Wednesday afternoon 4:00PM

Detective Nichols adds a note to the police file that Jack Holt is now the prime suspect. The detective did not explain why Jack Holt went from a person of interest to a prime suspect.

Wednesday afternoon 5:25PM

Detectives Nichols and Templeton go to Jack Holt's apartment to talk to him. Once again, there is no answer. They waited for two hours before deciding to return the next morning.

Thursday morning 6:15AM

Detectives arrive at the Quail Run apartments and wait out of sight for Jack Holt. As soon as Jack Holt leaves his apartment, the detectives confront him. When they show their badges and tell Jack Holt who they are, Jack refuses to talk. He tells them he is going into his apartment unless they intend to arrest him.

Detective Nichols called their lieutenant. Templeton waited outside Jack Holt's apartment to make sure he doesn't disappear. Detective Nichols explained the situation to their boss. They take Mr. Holt into custody as a person of interest. By refusing to talk, both detectives elevate him to a prime suspect based on his actions.

In the interrogation room at the precinct, he continued to invoke the Fifth Amendment, refusing to talk without a lawyer. On and off for four hours, the detectives continue to insinuate that his actions are not protecting him but are, in fact, hurting him. Jack Holt wouldn't talk to the detectives until he had legal representation.

After hours of badgering, they let Jack call the Public Defender's office.

The next day, Jackson Maynard petitions Judge Martin Shoemaker, a police-friendly judge, to extend holding Jack Holt for ninety-six hours. They also request a warrant to search his apartment and any storage areas, regardless of location. The judge grants both. He warns them he will not give an extension.

A CSI team went to the landlord of Jack Holt's apartment and served the search warrant. They informed the apartment manager that Mr. Holt was in custody.

I discovered nothing significant other than confiscating Jack Holt's toothbrush and a small glass of water. It was more than enough for DNA testing. Crime scene technicians rushed the samples to be tested.

I thought it was odd they had no evidence he had committed a crime. The only thing that ties him to the death of Maggie Stewart is her neighbor, Marilyn Pope, who identified him, sort of.

I remembered a statement in the autopsy report. It noted that the coroner found nothing under Maggie's fingernails that showed any violent act. I finished studying the police report and focused for a few minutes on photographs of both Maggie Stewart and Jack Holt. Maggie was a beautiful woman. A professional photographer took several photos of her. She had olive skin and stunning hazel eyes. Mr. Holt's face appeared disfigured on the left side from a blunt object. I studied the injuries on his face, trying to understand what had happened. When everything was complete, one fact was indisputable. His facial features were unnerving. It was odd there was no mention in the detective's case file about his facial features. Why would the detectives gloss over something as glaring as this man's facial disfigurement in their report? It made no sense. I called the county jail and set up a meeting at two in the afternoon to meet with Jack Holt. There must be something I overlooked, or something in those missing pages would explain their logic. I don't understand. Why was Jack Holt charged with these crimes? Something isn't right.

Chapter 10

Alexander Molina ~ Juror #9

I came to this country when I was two years old. And yes, my parents came here without apology. In fact, according to my parents, a wealthy farmer recruited our family to come to America to pick crops. I have no memories of my family's life in the remote mining town of San Francisco del Oro in the Mexican state of Chihuahua. The silver and copper mines were drying up, and the work was scarce. The wealthy farmers were hiring cheap labor and couldn't have cared less about my parent's legal status. For my parents, it was steady work, while for my siblings and me, it was an opportunity. We traveled between Las Cruces, New Mexico, and Sonoma County, California, picking all kinds of crops on every farm in New Mexico, Arizona, and California. It was doing dirty, backbreaking jobs that no one wanted. At a fortunate time, they found steady work and the opportunity that had eluded them in Mexico. It was an opportunity for my siblings and me to have a better life.

My parents taught themselves how to speak, read, and write in English. They insisted we learn both languages and read everything we get our hands on in both English and Spanish. More than once, my father told us that the only way out of poverty is an education. A lecture my siblings and I heard throughout our childhood. He told us that an educated mind was the only thing people couldn't take from us. I thought he was crazy when he insisted, we do well in school. As tired as they were, they did their best to help us do our homework. My older sister is a pediatric oncologist working in Los Angeles. My younger brother is an electrical engineer working in Sunnyvale, California. I teach and research social anthropology at Stanford University. My parents are deceased, but they gave us the opportunity to succeed. It boiled down to this; we had a choice to make our education an enjoyable experience or they would make us the most miserable Mexican kids in the world. They promised all three of us we would go to college. Our parents expected all of us to excel; that was nonnegotiable!

Tuesday, Day One, 5:27 PM

"I'm a professor of social anthropology. The science is more popular in Europe than in the United States," I told the jury.

"Are you an expert or something?" asked Hassan Saragana.

"Are you referring to my conversation with Mr. Eckert about bigotry?"

"Yeah. You were talking about bigotry."

"I was referring to a survey taken years ago," I responded. "There's no need to waste everyone's time. I'm not sure it's even relevant to what we're trying to do here today."

"Why don't you let us decide? I, for one, would love to hear what you're talking about. Marty Chu wondered if we were prejudging the defendant. "I don't want to send an innocent man to prison for life if I ignored something that could have been important."

"Me too," said Sara King.

"I agree," said Hassan Saragana.

"I'll be as brief as I can. A television network commissioned a research company to study the state of prejudice in America. The company polled ten thousand people across the United States. These people represented all social economic classes, races, education level, and gender." I noticed that Linda Sawyer has a frustrated expression on her face. I continued, "their method was interesting. The questions dealt with these issues. Are you biased toward people who are of a different race, gender, sexual orientation, disability, or religion? They planned another question in the following way:"

Without a word, Henry stands up, groans in disgust, then walks toward the window to watch it rain on the courthouse-parking garage.

"Please Henry, you're being disruptive," responded Hassan. "What he has to say is important."

"Where was I? Oh yeah, I remember. They asked people a series of questions in two ways. One question was how they felt about an issue. The other question was how that same person thought other people felt about the same issue."

"Where are you going with this?" asked Henry. "I don't see the relevance at all."

"Yes, this is relevant," Oscar responded to Henry's statement. "You are missing something. Please listen to what this man is saying. Go ahead, Alex. I remember reading an article in Scientific America about this subject."

"Pollsters asked about prejudices. When pollsters asked about prejudices, the respondents showed they were not prejudiced, with ninety percent of them giving such responses. Do you have prejudices toward people who are obese? The pollsters learned ninety-eight percent of the group of ten thousand were not."

"Henry, still staring out of the window says. "Could you please wrap this up? We have actual issues we need to be discussing."

"Henry, I tired of your unsolicited hurtful comments. Please stop it and let Alex finish," asked the foreperson.

"I'll be brief as possible," I answered. "When the pollsters asked the same question a different way, the answers were much different. Most people believe ninety percent of Americans are bigoted, but they themselves are not."

"Wrap it up, Alex," ordered Linda. "Jesus!"

"Why don't you sit your scrawny ass down and listen?" asked Kayla.

"Kayla," said the foreperson. "Please stop it! Go ahead, Alex."

"Okay, thank you. Based on how these people responded, they concluded Americans refused to admit their own bigotry. Yet, recognize other Americans were bigoted. The variation between the two questions was large. Over ninety percent of the people polled said they themselves have no prejudice toward others. Yet these same people recognized that most other Americans, over ninety percent, are bigoted. The polling company also posed this question. Who would you least want to work with? The number one answer was obese people at twenty-nine percent of those polled. The second highest response was people with a facial disfigurement. This group came in at twenty-four percent of the people polled."

After deliberating, some members of the jury became even more frustrated. At the request of most of the other jurors, I spent thirty minutes discussing the state of prejudice in America. The subject didn't sit well with Henry Keller, Linda Sawyer, and Ira McMillian. This added to the jury's weariness. The initial vote was ten guilty and two not guilty. During the deliberations, Kayla Rooney changed her vote to not guilty.

Henry and Linda's remarks undermine the ability of the foreperson. The remarks added an air of hostility in the jury room.

The foreperson shared her thoughts on the state of the jury. "It would be a mistake if we weren't fair about how we went about coming to a verdict. If your goal is to hurry this process along so you can get on with your life, there are two things you need to consider. Mr. Holt is on trial for murder. He at least deserves an in-depth conversation about the prosecution's case. I can see that some of you are in a hurry to get this over. I understand. We've been listening for a week about the circumstances around Maggie Stewart's murder. A few more days aren't asking too much. If we convict or acquit, we can sleep well knowing we have revisited the issues. We all have families and lives to go back to. I suggest we try our best to discuss the issues. Since we're on the topic of who voted guilty, I'm changing my vote from guilty to not guilty. The vote is now eight guilty and four are not guilty."

Henry told the jury he's in no hurry. If he has to stay another week, that's fine with him as long as we put that disgusting, perverted bastard in prison for life. His only regret is that the death penalty isn't an option. He demanded the four "not guilty" voters explain how they came to their absurd conclusions. Henry seemed angry, considering the task at hand. Henry's bullying didn't work on Oscar, Kayla, or me, but the foreperson took offense at his tone and posturing.

A muffled humming sound interrupts the conversation as Linda opens her purse and tries to excuse herself to the restroom. The foreperson reminds her that the judge and the bailiffs warned everyone about cellphones and computers not being allowed in the jury room. The judge ordered the jurors to surrender all electronic devices during deliberations. If there were urgent issues, the juror should tell the bailiff, and the bailiff will let them know if they receive a call. Linda stands up as she tells the foreperson she has no choice; she has to take the call. Linda answers the call and holds up her index finger, ignoring the foreperson. Kayla Rooney grabs the phone from Linda, turns it off, and slides it across the table to the foreperson.

Linda becomes incensed with Kayla, who remains calm while she stands up. Kayla is ten inches taller and fifty pounds heavier than Linda. She suggests Linda sit down and act like someone who gives a shit.

The foreperson asks the jury if there are other devices. No one answers. Janet knocks on the door, and when the bailiff answers, she gives the phone to the bailiff.

Hassan Saragana tells Henry that he's without question the rudest, most racist person he'd ever met. He insists Henry show respect to other members of the jury. Sara King, Mike Shepard, and Michael Eckert agreed with Hassan's comments.

Henry stands up and goes back to the window. "What the hell is happening? People get pissed about the most ridiculous things."

"Henry, I understand your frustration. I voted guilty because the evidence convinced me this guy raped and murdered that woman," said Michael Eckert. "You seem upset with people for reasons having nothing to do with our job. Please stop being so insulting toward people on this jury. It doesn't help." He turns to Linda Sawyer. "Linda, your actions aren't helping either. I understand you have an important job, but right now at this moment, we are trying to find justice for this man. For most of us here today, this is the single most important decision in our lives. I'm taking this job serious, and I find it offensive that you're in a hurry to get on with what you consider being more important things. All we've done since we came here to decide the fate of this man is to become more and more frustrated with each other. Can we just discuss the issues? Let's have enough respect for the other juror's opinions to listen without interrupting?"

"I agree with Michael," said Oscar Rosenthal. "Let's discuss the issues and only the issues. Let's look at this from the prosecution's case. Then let's look at the case the defense presented. Can we agree with that approach?"

The foreperson began, "The central question of the prosecution's case is straightforward. The victim is a wealthy, beautiful, and international famous model. They claim the defendant is a pathological liar, an alcoholic, and cannot keep a job. He has two convictions for DUI, and police took him into custody on suspicion of domestic violence. At the center of the prosecution's case are two simple questions. Did Maggie Stewart and Jack Holt have a romantic relationship? Did Maggie Stewart have sexual intercourse with the defendant? Does anyone have anything else to add?"

Marty Chu began sharing his thoughts: "The prosecution implied there was no way Maggie Stewart would have sex with Mr. Holt. To me, it's interesting the prosecution never came out and said that. It was only through innuendo that they conveyed the root of their case."

Ira McMillian added his comments. "For me, what sealed Jack Holt's case was that he's a habitual liar. You can't believe a word this guy says. He lied about getting injured while serving in the Army in combat. I'm a veteran, and what he did was inexcusable."

Henry, speaking from the window, said that Holt is beyond disgusting and made him ill. Henry took his seat at the table. "I suppose you will tell us that according to your new bullshit science, we're supposed to let him go free. You seem to forget he's a monster and if released will rape and murder again. Guaranteed."

"May I add something here? While I don't claim to be an expert on the subject, I don't understand what motivated Mr. Holt to say those things. I can say with reasonable certainty that in our culture there is a bias against those who have a significant facial deformity like Jack Holt. Does everyone agree with that assessment?"

"No," answered Henry, "I don't have a prejudice bone in my body. I resent that you're even implying that I do."

"As a nurse for the past twenty-five years, I think your statement is true," said the foreperson. "For the sake of this conversation, let's all agree, at least for now, that we have issues with his facial features. Dr. Molina, what point are you trying to make?"

"All I was trying to say was Mr. Holt could have been reframing his disfigurement to make it more socially acceptable."

"What?" asked Henry. "You've got to be kidding!"

"Jesus, what is wrong with you? Stop with your little horrible remarks," said the foreperson.

"I'm pointing out that Mr. Holt, as far as I know, didn't tell these lies for any personal gain. He wanted nothing more than acceptance. Did everyone see it the same way I did?" I looked at the other jurors. No one contradicted my statement, so I continued. "Circumstance motivates people to do some odd things. Most people don't do things without a reason."

Henry, standing at the window, turned around to face the other jurors. "Jack Holt is nothing but a gutless coward. I know a lot of soldiers who died in service in our country. His lies are disgusting."

Chapter 11

Jack Holt

"**Y**ou're here early, it's only four o'clock. You okay, brother?"

"Yeah," I answered as the guard locked the cell door behind me. "The judge invited the lawyers to her chambers to discuss one witness. We waited for thirty minutes. When they returned, the judge announced they were stopping and would reconvene tomorrow morning."

"That's cool, man. So, you get a little time off. How are you holding up?"

"The prosecution is wrapping up their case against me."

"And?"

"I'm screwed. My lawyer thinks I have a decent chance of beating the charges, but I think it's all over."

"I thought your lawyer was doing an excellent job for you?"

"I think he's doing the best he can to disprove the evidence against me, but that's not my problem."

"Oh, yeah?"

"I hope my lawyer discredits the prosecution's charges against me. My experiences tell me otherwise. Some of those people on the jury had me guilty before the trial even started."

"Do you think it was because of your face?"

"Is a frog's butt watertight?"

"Yeah man, I hear you. If I had sold grass to only a black or a Latino dude, I wouldn't be in this stinky ass jail. I sold pot to a freckle-faced gabacho puto from the suburbs, and that's why my sorry brown ass is sitting in this stinking jail."

Leto was lonely and talked nonstop. I didn't mind because he was a decent man, and I appreciated his company. We had a lot in common. It never occurred to me we had so much in common. We shared stories over dinner and even when we got back to our cell. At eight o'clock, I told my cellmate I had to get some sleep. I took half of a brown sugar pill and drifted off to be with my dreams. At least for the night, I'd be free of all of my worries.

• • • •

"Mr. Jack?" said Maggie as she looked across the pile of yellow onions in the produce section of Hernandez's Grocery store. "How nice to run into you."

"Well, hello Maggie, what a pleasant surprise. So, you're getting a little grocery shopping done?"

"Yeah, it's not my favorite thing to do. Hey, it's Saturday. My husband is out of town at a medical convention in San Diego. At least, that's what he told me. So here I am getting food I like to eat without listening to all his bullshit."

"I do the grocery shopping every Saturday morning. It doesn't take long. All I buy is the processed foods. Don't give me that look. Contrary to conventional wisdom, processed foods are wonderful for you. I'll have you know I read the labels. If it's high in sodium, fat, sugar, and especially a lot of chemicals, then I know I'm making a healthy choice. I hate cooking. I eat out as much as possible, but there are those junk food necessities that are a must when I get the urge."

"What's your favorite junk food?" asked Maggie.

"Ice cream, by leaps and bounds. Not just ice cream, but the high fat and high sugar creamy ice cream, you know the healthy stuff. Why is all the wonderful stuff so bad for you?"

"I knew we had something in common. I love any kind of ice cream, especially chocolate ice cream. Ah, God, that's good! There's one insignificant thing," said Maggie, looking up and down the aisle. "Ice cream doesn't love me back because I'm lactose intolerant. Every time I eat it; I get a dose of the galloping goodies."

"That just might be a little too much information."

"Sometimes when I'm home alone, I'll eat a gigantic bowl of ice cream knowing what will happen. If my husband finds out, he gets all worked up."

It was the third time we met. Unlike the first two meetings, this time, I felt most comfortable. I still wasn't sure how to take her. She had none of the usual body language of people who seem a little ill at ease because of my face. To be honest, I don't think she ever had any feelings like that. Her smile was captivating. I felt a deep sense of trust in her genuine hello. When she told me how nice it was to run into me, it wasn't superficial. Even with all her wonderful qualities, I still questioned her motives. I'm a little paranoid about people's reactions to my disfigured face.

From the time we first met in Homestead Park, Maggie liked me. She appreciated my going to Reggie's Coffee Shop and getting her a bottle of water and a few bar towels. She said it was the kindest act she'd received in a long time.

I was honest with myself. We even talked about why I was such a complete jerk when I was young. I explained that the reason my marriage fell apart was 100 percent my fault. It failed because I drank too much booze combined with years of self-loathing. I even told her about my estranged son. I let her fill in the gaps on why I don't have a relationship with him. There was nothing romantic in our relationship. The fact is that I wasn't too sure about her motives. I'm not putting myself down, but women like Maggie don't fall for guys who look like me. She's being almost too nice to me. What was she trying to prove?

When we talked, she appeared to be sincere. It was fine. I thought her fascination with me would get old and she'd move on. Whatever it was or wasn't, I would not let myself get suckered into something no matter how good-looking she is.

We talked in the produce section for an hour. Customers kept asking us to move so they could get by. We went to the in-store coffee shop and talked there for at least another hour. The fact was, we lost track of time as we imparted our opinions on what seemed to be a chain of meaningless topics. We didn't realize three hours had gone by; we laughed, continued talking for another hour before leaving.

"Is there any chance that you'd like to join me for dinner?"

"I'd love to, but I've got a lot of things to do tonight."

"I don't want to hurt your feelings, but Jack, you know, and I know, that's total B S. Come on, here's the deal you pick the restaurant, and I'll buy. Okay?"

"Well..."

"No, that's not true. I don't believe that you have to go. You want to have dinner with the most beautiful model in the world, perhaps even the entire solar system. I'm the model whose intelligence is only exceeded by her beauty. Come on, don't act like a complete nincompoop.

"All right."

"I knew you would. Now pick a joint."

· · · ·

"The Fourth Street Diner wasn't what I was envisioning when I ask you to choose a place to have dinner," said Maggie, "as she took her seat in the booth."

"I admit it's not much, but I come here two or three times a week and the food will knock your socks off. Besides, my ex and I used to live in the apartment upstairs when we first got married. It's been here for twenty years that I know of. My server is Olivia O'Toole, who I've known since she was our neighbor in the other upstairs apartment. She's like my stepmother only with an Irish temper and a vindictive nature."

"It is a cute little cafe, and I like the idea that it's a locally owned business. The bright orange neon sign over the entrance is a city landmark. God only knows how many times I've driven by here.

It never occurred to me to stop and try it out," said Maggie as she grabbed a photocopied menu. "What do you recommend?"

"Over the years I've tried everything, and it's all amazing. I get the same server, Olivia. She treats me like I'm her long-lost son. Over the years, we've had a kind of mother and son relationship spiced up a bit with her ex rated sense of humor. If my hair's messy, she'll straighten it out with her hand. Then make some off-the-cuff comment that's not repeatable. She was as much a mom to me as she was a server."

"Are you talking about me?" asked Olivia as she approached their table.

"Hi Olivia."

"Good evening, my dear. I'm so glad you've upgraded to a high-class hooker rather than all those cheap street tramps you bring in here."

"Real funny, Olivia. This is Maggie, a friend of mine, and she's not a hooker, but she is a high-class chick."

"Kiddo, it's not my place to judge you. To each their own, you know? Whatever you want me to believe, hey, I'm cool," answered Olivia, winking at Maggie. "Nice to meet you, my dear."

"I love this place," said Maggie.

"Thank you, we're glad you came with one of our favorite customers," said Olivia. "Can I get you something to drink?"

"Do you have a nice Cabernet Sauvignon?" asked Maggie.

"We have a great medium-priced Italian Cabernet called Antinori Villa Toccana vintage 2013. It's five dollars a glass or twenty-two for the bottle. It's less if you buy the bottle."

"Does that sound okay to you, Jack?"

"Sure."

"We'll take the bottle," Maggie told Olivia.

We eased into the evening, taking in the little cafe's ambience. Maggie talked about her childhood in Sacramento, and I talked about all the books I've read over the past year. She must have thought what a poor bastard I was for reading so much.

"If I'm wrong about bringing this up, please let me know," said Maggie. "I couldn't help but notice how many people stare at you. I don't know about you, but when men gawk at me, it pisses me off to no end. When people gawk at you, doesn't it bug the hell out of you?"

"People have been staring at me for thirty years. Sometimes I think they can't help themselves. Sometimes they sneak a peek, thinking I won't notice. As strange as it sounds, some people become captivated by my appearance. God only knows what's going through their shallow little minds."

"I think it's so rude," said Maggie.

"Yeah, I agree. I ignore them, but I have to admit I have a little fun at their expense. I stare back and it creeps them out of them big time. Everyone notices my face. Most people have better things to do than to gawk at me."

"Is it impolite to ask what happened?"

"Nah, not at all." I gave her an abridged version of the accident that killed my father and both of my sisters. We talked about my mother's health struggles that resulted from the accident. I told Maggie about the financial troubles that my mother and I went through until she had no choice but to declare bankruptcy. We were at the mercy of Social Security and state-funded insurance. I told Maggie that my mother didn't die from the injuries from the accident. She died from worrying about the finances and what would become of me.

I asked Maggie about her life.

"As strange as it sounds, I have a very similar situation and one that turned out to be just as detrimental as issues you've confronted. My problem is like the other side of the same coin. It began when I started developing breast. I was about fourteen years old when boys started looking at me. It got creepy when old men started noticing my breast when I was fifteen. Men checking out my ass every time I go out in public. My parents are the reason I look like I look If they want to compliment someone on how beautiful I am, they should tell my mom and dad."

"It never occurred to me that a woman would feel that way," I responded. "To be honest, I never gave the negative side of it any thought. I just assumed that women would kind of like the attention for how beautiful they are." Maggie never considered the issues I confronted on almost a daily basis.

"We get gawked at by people for different reasons. I have a distinct advantage. There are definite advantages to being good looking. Men staring at me and concluding that I'm stupid because I'm easy on the eye make me angry as hell."

I hadn't thought about it in a long time, but Maggie's comments made me remember when I went through puberty, and how everything changed. I was reluctant to talk about it, but she seemed to understand. "After the accident, I was a cute little boy crippled in a terrible accident. Then, after I went through puberty, everything turned on a dime. I changed into a drooling creep. Some thought I was a pervert who was always stocking girls. I learned early on to be cautious around the opposite sex."

"Would it be disingenuous if I acted surprised about that? That day in the park for two seconds, your appearance startled me. Then you backed away and gave me a lot of room.

"It gets old, I know where you're coming from. Maybe it's kind of normal?"

"Who's kidding who? Being beautiful has made a lot of things possible. I've had good fortune, but if I could be less of an attraction and appreciated more for who I am, that would be terrific. Sometimes I feel like I'm nothing more than a slab of meat. When I was a working model, I weighed one hundred and ten pounds when my manager first mentioned that I should lose some weight. That was the first time anyone ever told me something like that. As a kid, I bought into all the glamor nonsense. They encouraged me to smoke, saying it would help me keep the weight off. When I was a model, there was always that one thing that wasn't right about me. After fourteen years of being a successful model, I was an emotional mess. Modeling was alluring and glamorous, and also the worst mistake of my life. In a single shoot, I made more money than both of my parents did in a year, yet I was miserable. Five years ago, I retired from my modeling career and set out to do something else. That's when I met my husband, which was the second biggest mistake in my life."

"I'm sorry," I said.

"Eh, well, what can I say?" answered Maggie.

"That's most likely what my ex-wife thought about marrying me. I can say without reservation that our divorce was one hundred percent my fault. The only surprising thing about my marriage was that she put up with me for as long as she did."

"You don't hear that often."

"I'm not proud of some things I did in my life. When you have a face like mine, no one gives you an operating manual. My mother and I didn't know how to deal with our physical problems. I was feeling so sorry for myself because of the way I looked, I couldn't make room for anything else. As for my former wife, I just couldn't understand what she saw in me. I drank too much and felt sorry for myself too much and wasn't a suitable husband or much of a father. She did the right thing by divorcing me and moving to Portland."

"When was the last time you saw your son?"

"When he was four years old when my ex left me. He will turn eighteen on his next birthday. She did the right thing for herself and our son. There are mistakes people make that are irreconcilable. I heard she married an affable guy and a wonderful role model for our son."

Olivia seemed to appear out of nowhere. "Can I interest you in dessert?" she said as she straightened my hair, then resting her hand on my left shoulder.

"I'm fine, Olivia," I answered. "As usual, the dinner was just great." I patted her hand.

"Saying the dinner was amazing is a total understatement. This cafe is a hidden treasure. Thank you. Would you mind telling me where the lady's room is?"

"Right over there, sweetheart," answered Olivia, pointing to a door near the entrance.

"I'll have an espresso," said Maggie as she got up from her chair.

"You know, an espresso sounds like it will hit the spot," I said. "I'll have one too."

"If you'll excuse me," said Maggie as she left the table.

When Maggie returned from the restroom, she seemed upset. She made me promise not to say anything or do anything before she'd tell me. After I promised, she shared what had happened to her in the restroom. While washing her hands, Olivia came in, locking the door behind her, then reiterated that she was my dear friend. She told Maggie there would-be harsh repercussions if she was using me. She guaranteed Maggie that payback would be hell. Olivia told her I was one of the nicest men she'd ever known, and she didn't want to see me get hurt. Just before Olivia left the restroom, she told Maggie that she holds grudges, and payback can be pure hell. I told Maggie that Olivia was as much my mother as she was a server. I explained when my former wife and I were first married; we lived upstairs in an apartment across the hall from Olivia. Olivia has seen me at my worst and my best, and she still was my friend.

A few days later, while having dinner there again, Olivia and I talked at length about the friendship between Maggie and me. I swore we were just friends.

I know I'm dreaming, but it feels good. At the end of dinner, we drank our espresso. Maggie studied me for the longest time and then told me she loved me. She understood the stress the trial was putting me through and told me she loved me more than she'd ever loved anyone.

Chapter 12

Joe Hammer

For the first time in a long time, I had a good night's sleep. Except I couldn't get the police report off my mind. Something didn't add up. I saw nothing that proved my client's guilt. I called Jackson Maynard and asked him if we could meet for breakfast. To my surprise, he agreed, provided we didn't meet anywhere near his office.

• • • •

I arrived at Denny's near my apartment in the northern suburbs. Jackson had his nose stuck in the Wall Street Journal when I arrived at his table. "Good morning."

"And good morning to you," he answered without putting the paper down. "Give me a few seconds, I want to finish this article on making authentic Mexican hot sauce."

I got the server's attention and ordered a cup of coffee.

"Hi Joe. Before we begin, I want to tell you that never in a million years did I ever think I'd see you as a defense attorney. Especially a lawyer working for the Public Defender's office."

"I know. What can I say, I got lucky?"

"What was so urgent that we had to meet for coffee?"

"I read the police report and the coroner's autopsy report of Maggie Stewart. I get it Jackson; you're like everyone else and think I'm the biggest asshole lawyer that ever lived. Admittedly, I deserved my terrible reputation. After reading the police and autopsy reports many times to see if I was missing something. It doesn't add up. Am I missing something?"

"Joe, what are you getting at?"

"Jackson, I don't have any other way to put this. What the hell is going on with Jack Holt? You have no evidence my client committed the crimes you've charged him with. His left arm and hand have atrophy. Theirs is no way he could have strangled Maggie Stewart. All the personal feelings toward me aside, I'm asking you as one professional to another. What's going on?"

"What are you saying, Joe?"

"It would be impossible for my client to kill that woman by strangulation. He cannot strangle a fly. To be honest with you, it looks to me like the Eric asked you to convict my client, knowing full well he's innocent."

Jackson takes a drink of his coffee. "Joe, I thought you were a talented lawyer. When I worked for you, I learned more than from anyone I'd ever worked with. I also thought you treated people terribly. You were embarrassing to work with. Not only should they have disbarred you, but they should have also charged you with wrongful prosecution for the way you handled the conviction of Miguel Acosta."

"You're right. The similarities between Miguel Acosta and Jack Holt are much more than a coincidence I hope that Eric Warren didn't ask you to convict a man you know is innocent because he has some agenda."

"Are you accusing me of wrongful prosecution?"

"I'm saying you have no evidence my client committed these crimes. These charges are bullshit, and you know it. I committed a crime when I prosecuted Mr. Acosta. I lost my license to practice as a result, and I'm still puzzled why the DA didn't bring charges against me. The similarities between Miguel Acosta's case and the case against Jack Holt are similar."

"Okay, Joe, I've heard enough. If you're concerned, you have an obligation as an officer of the court to bring this situation to the judicial disciplinary committee. As for Jack Holt, he's as guilty as anyone I've ever prosecuted in my career. For your information, I will get great satisfaction in putting him away for the rest of his life. Before you waste my time with these ridiculous accusations, you'd better do your homework, or I'll be taking you to the disciplinary committee. Trust me, Joe, I'll have no issues putting you away for a long time. I don't understand how Judge Horton let you practice law again. It defies any sense of decency. I think we're done."

• • • •

After my meeting with Jackson Maynard, I went to the Marsh County Detention Center to introduce myself to my client. When I arrived at the visitor center, I noticed a sign above the entrance: "Welcome to Consolidated Prisons America (CPA)." A reminder that Marsh County sold the facility to a private prison corporation. It was a very profitable ten-year contract for the private for-profit prison company to operate the detention center. One condition of the sale was that the jail must meet current federal standards for prisons. I noticed after entering the facility that the CPA had done nothing. The facility looked worse and had a persistent stench of stale urine.

The first person I met was an old guard named Benny Easley, who I had known for years. After we talked for a few minutes, he wasn't aware that I had been disbarred. I saw no reason to correct him; it wasn't like I was lying. To be honest, it was nice seeing someone from my former life who wasn't telling me what a jerk I was. After a few minutes of talking, I told the guard I was there to see Jack Holt.

"Hold on a minute, Joe let me have your guy brought to the holding cell. I'll escort you over there when he's there," said the guard. "You won't have a hard time putting this nutcase away."

"What makes you say that? Did he admit to killing that woman?"

"He said nothing to me. Is there any truth to the rumor that you made some kind of arrangement with a guy to spy on that creep?"

"I can't confirm or deny that rumor," I answered.

"I gotta tell ya, Joe, he makes my skin crawl. He's one strange look'n dude who has an attitude, if you know what I mean? The longer I work here, the better I know who's guilty and who isn't. He's one guilty son-of-a-bitch for sure."

It had been a while since I'd walked through a prison. I'd forgotten how every sound resonates through the building. As we approached the temporary holding room, the stench of urine was almost unbearable. "What's with the urine smell? How can you stand it?"

"I'm told they can't figure it out, but I'm not sure of that. Something tells me it's the budget. Anyway, it might be hard to believe, but you get used to it and the smell goes away," the guard answered. "I haven't smelled it in over a year. Here ya go Joe if you need anything, or things get out of hand hit the red button by the door."

I walked into the holding cell and smiled at my new client without saying a word. Jack Holt was sitting handcuffed to the metal table. I looked at him while putting my index finger to my mouth, signaling to him not to say anything. I listened as the sound of guards' footsteps faded.

"Hello, I'm Joe Hammer. I'm with the public defender's office. I don't know if you heard or not, but I'm your new lawyer," It surprised me that my client's facial features were worse than the mug shots portrayed. "So how are you doing?"

"Other than being in here, I'm fine," answered Jack Holt. "What happened to the other lawyer?"

"Some workloads got moved around and I have you as my client. Are they treating you okay in here?"

Jack shrugged his shoulders. "It's a jail. What can I say?"

"I should know this, but I don't. What did the judge set your bail at?"

"A million bucks, I guess he thought I'd run off and disappear into the crowd."

The irony of that statement flew ten feet over my head. "Before we get started, do you need anything? Do you have any special needs like prescriptions or stuff like that? How about a book or something?"

"A book? That's great. Is there any chance you could get me Slouching Towards Bethlehem, by Joan Didion? While you're at it, could you get me a small hot latte with one sugar?"

"Consider it done, Jack. Let me explain what my job is. If you already know this, I apologize, but I want to say it, anyway. Some people get confused about the job of a defense lawyer. In America, an accused person regardless of the crime is innocent until proven guilty. I'm not here to prove your innocence. I'm here to defend you against the prosecution who thinks you're guilty. To have a successful defense, the accused and the lawyer must be honest and open with each other. My job is to discredit the prosecution's case against you. It's important to remember you are innocent until proven guilty. If there is any doubt, the jury must acquit. Here's the deal about any case before the court, lawyers often rewrite the truth during the trial."

As we talked, I couldn't help but notice my client seemed indifferent toward his situation. Debating whether I should tell him about the judiciary panel disbarring me two years before. It was too early. Besides, I don't know this guy, and I'm trying to be fair.

As I was trying to have a conversation, I was becoming frustrated. He wasn't making a good first impression. I questioned the ethics of defense attorneys who defend guilty clients. 'Am I missing something? Before meeting Jackson this morning, I would have bet my client was being set up to take the wrap for someone else. I'm not so sure of my intuition as I used to be. What happens if they acquit this guy? What if he goes out and rapes and kills another woman?' I wondered if I could live with myself.

After twenty years of being a prosecutor, I had to remind myself that I was a defense attorney. One of those low-life lawyers I despised and considered scum of the earth. I believed that the guy sitting in front of me was as guilty as sin. My stomach churned, and I didn't have Pepto-Bismol. I found myself in a predicament. Why the hell would Judge Horton put me in such a lose/lose situation? Was there something going on that I didn't know? I got lost in my thoughts.

"Are you okay?" asked my client.

"I'm sorry," I responded, not hearing what he asked.

"Is everything okay? You're like zoning out."

"Yeah, I'm sorry," I answered. I'd decided that if I'm to be in this profession, I have to be honest. "I wasn't sure how to tell you. There's only one-way for you and me to be successful, we have to be honest and open with each other. I have to tell you that a week ago I was mixing paint at Hector's Home Improvement Center off Rosemont Avenue. Hector's hired me two years ago; I was unemployed and being disbarred as a prosecuting attorney. Losing my license to practice law because I was more interested in personal growth than being a professional lawyer. Throughout my entire legal career, my personality has not been the best. What I'm trying to say is I've been an obnoxious, condescending jerk who most people hated."

"Okay, that's dandy. Why are you telling me this?"

"It's important you know everything about me. The fact is, I was the single most disliked person practicing law in this state. During the hearing to disbar me, no one came to my defense. It was like my colleagues stood on the shoreline and took great pleasure in seeing me drown. You need to understand what I'm telling you. Last week, after reminding me what an asshole I am, a judge gave me an opportunity to defend you with some caveats. Until your trial is over, you are my only client. So now you're up to date on me. Questions?"

"Well, I suppose that's nice to know on some level. When it gets right down to the bottom line, I only hope you're a talented lawyer?"

"Yeah, well, at least I think so. There are many people who aren't too happy about me returning to the profession. You're my first client as a defense attorney."

"Since I don't have any money and you're my only option, I guess you'll have to do."

"I promise I'll do my best; I won't give you a line of lawyer bullshit, but you have to tell me everything. With one giant exception the case against you is circumstantial, and I don't understand how the DA charged you with anything. There is the matter of your semen being inside the victim's vagina. That's some serious evidence."

"I understand."

"I'm not trying to insult your intelligence, but I will start with some basic advice. Okay?"

"Sure."

"Keep your mouth shut. Don't talk to anyone except me. Even if your closest relatives come here and ask you what's going on, don't say a word, nothing! I worked as a prosecutor for my entire career. I can tell you they can and will use anything you say against you. Do you understand what I'm saying? No prosecutor in their right mind will ever admit this, but they are under enormous pressure for convictions. The unwritten law of the land that every legislator and prosecutor will deny. The private prison industry lobby is demanding more convictions and longer sentences. All being done under the pretense of law and order and saving taxpayer money. They'll never admit it. If you even mention it, you'll make it on someone's shit list, and that's not a good thing. Trust me, Jack, there are big time financial reasons they want your sorry ass in prison for a long time."

"Okay."

"This is important, I heard a rumor that the prosecution will plant a snitch. They made a deal with some guy promising that if he finds out anything they can use, he'll get a 'get out of jail free' card. Yes, they can do that and yes, they use that information to put you away for a long time. I know I sound like a broken record, but I can't stress this point enough. Keep your mouth shut. Be careful who you talk to, what you say and what you talk about. Questions?"

"No."

"I read the police report that outlines the prosecution's case against you. Here's my interpretation of their strategy. My initial reaction is you're guilty because guys who look like you are easy. Keep in mind all I know about you is what I read in your police report file. The prosecution will pass you off as a pervert who has a drinking problem. A guy who has had several accusations against him for unwanted sexual advances."

"You realize that is total bullshit, right?"

"I have no doubt about your innocence, but the 'That's Bullshit' defense doesn't go over well in a court of law. Our justice system revolves around affordability. If you have the financial means to hire an experienced defense lawyer, you'll have a reasonable chance of having a good outcome, even if you're guilty as hell. If you're poor, regardless of color, you're screwed. We're all taught to believe that our courts are fair-minded, even though justice is blind. Here's the truth, prosecutors want convictions by any means necessary. To them the poor people are low hanging fruit even if they have to pander to the jury's fears, they'll do it in a heartbeat. Remember the truth is subjective all they want is convictions. I know these guys because I used to be one of them. The lead prosecutor, Jackson Maynard, was my understudy when he started practicing law. He will take the easiest way to make sure his team gets a conviction. Everything they do is to get a conviction by whatever means necessary."

"So, you're saying I'm screwed?"

"The case against you is circumstantial except for the autopsy. So, let's start by discussing how your semen ended up inside the victim. Don't get pissy with me, but I have to ask you hard questions. Some questions because I don't know the answer. Other questions are to hear your response. Remember, we're on the same team. Can you tell me how your semen ended up inside Mrs. Stewart?"

"The usual way. We had sex two times on Friday morning, the same day she disappeared. Once in the morning and again the same day after lunch, two hours before she disappeared."

"Was it consensual sex?"

Jack looked at me for a few seconds. "Yeah, it was not only consensual, but it was also her idea. Believe it or not, I'm not a rapist."

"Why did the prosecution conclude it was sexual assault?"

"Are you kidding?"

"No, I'm not kidding at all. I'm serious, I need to hear it from you. Why do you think the prosecution believes you raped and murdered her?"

Jack stares at me. "My facial features."

"The detectives said you refused to talk to them without a lawyer being present. Is that correct? And if it is, why wouldn't you talk to them?"

"The first time they came, I didn't open the door. I knew the instant they saw my face they'd quit looking elsewhere. I could tell by their expressions when they approached me the next morning, they'd found their man. There's only one outcome from this trial."

"What's that?"

Jack shook his head in frustration. "Come on, man, quit screwing with me. If your future is riding on my acquittal, you're in trouble. If my case goes to trial, there is no chance in hell of an acquittal I'm on a one-way trip to prison for the rest of my life. You know that and I do too. You said to be honest, well there it is, pal. Here's a truth bomb, I'm screwed, and you know it."

I listened as he let out his feelings. It was going on and on. "Are you done feeling sorry for yourself?"

"You just went through a shit load of preaching about being honest. You sound just like a lawyer. When push comes to shove, you don't want to hear what I have to say. Look, I'm not trying to be difficult, but the fact is there's no way in hell I will get an acquittal."

"At this moment, I don't know whether I'll get you off. Okay, pal? That's the bottom line. The only question you have to answer at the moment is this. 'Do you want me to represent you in this case or not?' That's all you need to tell me, yes or no."

"Either way. I couldn't care less."

"It's your life," I answered, putting files into my briefcase. "It's a free country, and you can do as you please."

"Do you think you can get me off?"

"Beats me, Jack. I understand where you're coming from. I also understand the case against you is about your facial disfigurement. There's no getting around it. I think the odds of an acquittal are overwhelming against you. All I can tell you is that nobody will be more dedicated than me. Believe me when I tell you I'll do my best at either getting the charges against you dismissed or getting you acquitted."

"I'm telling you I didn't kill Maggie. Before God I swear, I didn't kill her."

"Okay, I don't care. It's my job to make sure the prosecution doesn't have a case against you. To do that, you need to work with me."

"You may not care but I sure as hell care! If you don't believe me, then what's the goddamn point? I did not rape or kill Maggie. As hard as it is for people to believe or understand, we were in love. After her divorce from the psycho doctor husband, we were getting married. Why is that so hard to believe?" A tear ran down Jack's cheek.

I tapped my knuckles on the table while I listened to my client. Then I realized I had come to this meeting thinking like a prosecutor. My client was most likely telling the truth. "What happened to your face?"

"When I was eight years old my parents, sisters, and I were on our way home from a camping trip. We were just east of San Bernardino when one of those customized off-road pickup trucks hit us head-on. Do you know the truck I'm talking about?"

"Yeah, I think so. Is it one of those trucks that you almost need a stepladder to get in the cab?"

"That's it. We'd just turned a corner when one of those trucks plowed into my dad's side of our car. The two guys in the truck were drunk. Neither of them got a scratch. The truck killed my father and my two sisters."

"What about your mother?"

"She survived but was a paraplegic. The collision pushed her legs into her abdomen. She also had a colectomy where doctors removed her colon, bowel, and rectum. She had to have a colostomy bag for the rest of her life."

"I'm sorry."

"As for what caused my problems. When the truck hit us, it jostled around the inside of our car. In a nutshell, my injuries happened when my mother's head slammed into my head, somehow causing the seventh cranial nerve to shut down. I was eight when the traffic accident happened. That's why I'm paralyzed on the left side of my face. Between the paralysis and the atrophy, the upper left side of my body leans to the left. Does that answer your question?"

"Hold on a second. You said atrophy?"

"Yes."

"Where do you have atrophy?"

"In the left side of my neck, both shoulders, my left arm and hand."

"Okay Jack, help me out here. What's the difference between paralysis and atrophy?"

"The muscles in the left side of my face are paralyzed, so they don't move at all."

"Show me your arms?"

Jack, being handcuffed to the metal table, did the best he could to show his arms and hands. "Can you see the difference in muscle size between the two arms and hands?"

"I'll be damned. There's a lot of difference," said Joe as he examined both arms and hands. He put his index finger out as if he were pointing. "Jack squees my finger with your right hand."

Jack squeezed as hard as he could.

"Okay, that's enough. Do the same thing with your left hand.

Jack squeezed Joe's finger with his left hand.

Joe noticed a stark difference in strength between Jack's hands. The difference was shocking. In fact, the difference, at least in Jack's mind, made it impossible for him to strangle Maggie. He wrote a note to himself to recheck Maggie Stewart's autopsy report. Joe looked up at Jack. "Yeah. So only your mother and you survived?"

"If you want to call it that. She was in constant pain for the rest of her life?"

"What happened to the people in the other car?"

"Like I said, neither of those bastards got hurt. The police arrested the driver for DUI. The driver served two years in jail. My mother sued both of them, but you can't squeeze blood out of a turnip. To top it off, the bastard's truck was uninsured. I got out of the hospital after nine months and stayed with my Aunt Margaret. My mother got out of the hospital six months after I did, but she could never care for herself. Because of our medical insurance and my father's life insurance policy, we were at first doing okay.

Everything has their limits, and so did the medical insurance. We had a nurse that came to our house twice a week for two years until the insurance company dropped us. When I was eleven, I started taking care of my mother. Before school, and after school, I would change her colostomy bag and give her a sponge bath. At first it was uncomfortable, but I was proud to have helped her. If we hadn't had all the money issues, I think she would still be alive today. We had no other source of income except a meager social security check each month. We were destitute and living on the good graces of other people. Mom's health situation was expensive, her medical needs depleted everything we had. We moved into a studio apartment after selling our house." Jack stopped to take a few deep breaths. "Selling our house and getting state sponsored health care gave us three more years, but it wasn't enough. One morning I went to my mother's bedroom to feed her breakfast, change her bag, and clean her up before going to school. Unfortunately, I discovered she had died during the night. In a way it was the worst, best thing that happened to her since the accident. After losing everything we had and surviving on the good graces of friends and family, she found peace. If I live to be a hundred, I'll always think of those years of helping my mother as the best years of my life. She' s buried alongside my father and my sisters. I hope she found peace."

Chapter 13

Linda Sawyer ~ Juror #6

My boss had the creepiest comb-over I've ever seen. He also had a disgusting habit of touching me with his wandering hands. He always apologized and claimed it was an accident. I noticed something about his so-called accidental touching. He always touched my breasts, my crotch, or my ass. The last time he grabbed my ass; I threatened to turn him in to Human Resources. That happened two weeks ago, and I haven't seen or heard from him since.

Rumors went around the office about a corporate restructure. I didn't buy my boss's explanation. Like everyone else, I knew what it meant; layoffs sound more palatable. Right in the middle of all this office drama, I received word that I would have to be on jury duty. After ten days, they selected me to be on a jury for the biggest trial in many years. This news was devastating. Right in the middle of the biggest restructuring in our company's history, and I have to be on a damn jury. I went to my boss for help to get me off this jury. When I arrived, his administrative assistant said he was too busy to meet me. I ignored her and entered his office unannounced.

"Let me call you back." He listened for a few seconds. "Yeah, I understand. My apologies but I need to hang up."

I stood in front of his desk.

"Linda, it's customary to knock on my door before entering. What do you want?"

"The people who run the jury system sent me a letter letting me know I have to report for jury duty next Monday," I reached across his desk to give him the letter. "Can you help get me off."

"You asked me this ten days ago, and I wrote them a letter. They must have ignored it."

"Are you serious? I can't be sitting on a jury while everything here falls apart. What will happen to my job?"

"What day do you have to start jury duty?"

"Next Monday morning. Is there anything you can do to help me get out of this? What would happen if I just didn't show up?"

"Something tells me it wouldn't be the best idea. Winslow, Morris, and Baker Investment Bankers has a lot of pull with the county and state officials. We're the largest source of funding for the city, Marsh County, and the state? Every once in a while, we can throw our weight around and get our way if it's in our best interest. Let me make some calls and see what I can do. How does that sound?"

"Thank you, Doug. Anything you can do would help."

"That's why I'm here. Why don't you run along, and I'll get in touch with you when I hear something?"

I got pissed off. Did that little creep just tell me to 'run along!' This is payback for threatening him for grouping my ass on purpose. I sucked it up. "I'd appreciate anything you can do,"

"On your way out, tell Dolores to come in here."

There was something about his choice of words, the condescending way he dismissed me. "Sure, no problem," I answered as I walked out of his office. I told Dolores that he needed to see her right away. She got up, grabbed a notebook, and went into his office. I watched as she entered, closing the door behind her. The latch didn't connect; the door reopened halfway. Despite my refusal to eavesdrop, anger consumed me.

"Linda said you wanted to see me."

"Why did you let her burst into my office?"

"I tried to stop her, but she wouldn't listen."

"I don't give a good goddamn if it's my mother and my grandmother waiting to see me. No one bursts into my office. Got it? No one! If that happens again, clean your desk out."

"I'm sorry, it won't happen again."

"Sit down. I want you to read this file to see if there are any mistakes. While you're doing that, I need to make a quick phone call."

"Yes, sir."

"This is Doug, is Mr. Winslow in?"

There was silence for a very long time. I felt awkward eavesdropping.

"Hello Mr. Winslow. The woman we were discussing burst into my office. It turns out we have a little luck. She's on jury duty starting this coming Monday. I don't know how long she'll be there, but she'll be out of our hair for a while."

There was a pause. What he said was unbelievable. Losing my job was not an option.

"See you on Monday. Thank you."

• • • •

"That's correct. You asked me why I voted not guilty," answered Oscar Rosenthal. "I agree with Dr. Molina. I feel this man, whether he's guilty or innocent, deserves an in-depth discussion of the facts of the case. For the record, I think there is merit in his observations from an anthropological point of view. That was something I had never considered."

I noticed Henry listening to my comments as he stood by himself, looking out of the window. After I finished, Henry turned around and addressed the jury. "Come on everyone! You cannot be buying any of this nonsense. Who are you trying to impress? No one in this room has the slightest idea what you're talking about. What is an anthropological point of view? Who even cares? How does it relate to locking this creep up in prison? It sounds like a bunch of mumbo-jumbo, if you ask me. It doesn't matter what you think you know. What's going on with you people? Open your eyes, it's simple. Jack Holt obsessed over Maggie Stewart. He stocked that poor woman. She was good looking, and he wanted to have sex with her, it's that simple. After he raped her, he murdered her to cover his tracks. That's all you need to know. It's as simple as that. All that talk about anthropology is ridiculous. We're wasting our time talking," Henry takes his seat at the table. "I can't believe you're talking about all this crap. If you keep it up this guy will walk."

"Henry are you finished?" asked the foreperson.

"You know what? No, I'm not. Does anyone in this room understand what Ockham's razor is?"

Oscar Rosenthal and Alex Molina nodded. They understood.

"That figures. Ockham's razor is the assumption that states when you have competing theories, the one with the fewest assumptions is the right one."

"Sir, your definition of Ockham's razor isn't quite correct," said Alex Molina.

"But you get my point?"

There is a knock on the door. The foreperson looked surprised as she got up and opened the door. A cafeteria worker with a cart full of snacks is at the door.

"We were just getting started. Let's take five before we continue," said the foreperson.

· · · ·

"How are you two doing?" asked Henry, who joined a conversation between Marty and Hassan.

"Just fine," answered Marty Chu. "How are you?"

"I'm tired of being here, that's for sure. This jury has no chance of reaching a verdict. The 'not guilty,' people will not be changing their minds."

"We have to keep trying," responded Hassan. "I understand the judge is fussy about hung juries."

"She's just saying that stuff, so she won't have to go through another trial," said Henry. "Trust me, there's nothing she can do. The decision the jury makes is final."

"Are you sure that's right?" said Marty. "I think she can order us back into deliberations if she wants to."

"Trust me guys, the judge has to live with whatever we decide," said Henry. "She's just trying to bully a decision. What do you guys think of the foreperson?"

"She's okay," answered Hassan. "I sure wouldn't want her job."

"Yeah, I agree," said Marty. "She seems okay to me too."

"I wish I could agree but she just doesn't have any leadership skills," said Henry. "If we had a solid leader, we'd all be home right now, and that bastard would be on his way to prison."

"Maybe so, who knows," answered Hassan.

"Can I ask you a question?" asked Henry to Hassan,

"Sure, why not?"

"Are the deliberations cramping your style? I noticed you didn't pray yesterday afternoon."

Hassan grins in disbelief. "Are you serious? If you remember I already said I'm not Muslim."

"Muslims could quit?"

"Beats me. I didn't quit being a Muslim because I never was a Muslim. My father was never a Muslim and my mother is Scotch-Irish, brought up in the Methodist Church. For the record, my parents are like me and my wife, devout non-believers."

"Henry, if you're keeping track, I'm a Buddhist and a democrat," said Marty Chu.

"Gosh, Henry, as always it was delightful talking to you," said Hassan. "We should get back to our chairs."

• • • •

I overheard Linda saying, "Don't associate me with Henry. The other jurors have been talking about Henry this and Linda that. I don't understand. All I want is for this shit show to be over as soon as possible. I'm tired as hell and I want to go back to work to see if I have a job. Who cares about the guy who's on trial. I'd change my vote in a heartbeat to get out of here.

The foreperson returned from the restroom and take her seat. She looked at the clock and called the jury back to order. A few minutes passed before everyone sat down.

"Where do we go from here?" Linda asked. "Before the break, Henry made some important comments. Let's not make this a long-drawn-out process, especially since it's so obvious what happened. Some of us have lives and I for one would like to get all of this behind me."

"Let's face it." said Michael Eckert. "Jack Holt has lived a troubled life since getting the injuries to his face. I understand, children can be so cruel, it's no wonder he turned out the way he did. He had a drinking problem. When he loses his temper, he sounds a little paranoid, and to top it off he's a compulsive liar. I get it. I understand why he is the way he is. When you boil it down, there is little doubt in my mind that he's guilty. This case is simple there is no other reasonable conclusion. I realize the two of you want to share with the rest of us how smart you are, that has nothing to do with this case."

"Madam foreperson, may I respond to that comment?" asked Alex Molina.

"Sure, go ahead."

"I have serious questions about the prosecution's theories. To me they don't stack up," said Alex Molina.

"What is it you don't understand?" asked Henry Keller. "Maybe I can help you?"

"Excuse me, please hold on a minute," said the foreperson. "There are a few people who are certain the defendant is guilty. You might be right. That's why we are here to discuss the details of this case with an open mind," She looks at Henry, Ira, and Linda. "You are certain of the conclusion you've drawn. You don't seem to be open-minded about listening to what other jurors have to say. Please, for the sake of this process, be more open-minded. Henry, would you like to rephrase your question?"

"No," answered Henry. "We're deciding the fate of a man accused of rape and murder. I have no problem sending this man to prison for the rest of his life. I know he's guilty."

Ignoring Henry's comments, "Why don't we discuss the testimony given during the trial from the beginning to the end?" suggested Kayla.

"There you go, someone's thinking," said Marty. "It can't take that long there were only a handful of witnesses who testified. We can even ask the court clerk for the transcripts of the witness's testimony if we need to. We can ask for them, right?"

"Yes, we can ask for the transcripts if we feel the need," answered Kayla.

"Just to make sure I'll ask the bailiff," said the foreperson.

I listened to everyone discussing their opinions as to the guilt or innocence of Jack Holt. The black woman sitting next to me is making sense. I don't like her big mouth and aggressive behavior, but she does sometimes make sense. Although I agree with Henry in his assessment of the defendant's guilt, other than that, I think he's a total jackass. I'm so tired of being here, worrying whether I'll have a job when this is over.

Chapter 15

Jack Holt

"**H**ey Leto, are you asleep?"

"Are you kidding? With all the noise that guard made bringing you down the hall," Leto responded as he lay in his bunk with his eyes shut. "That pendejo guard woke everyone up. Why are you so late?"

"The shuttle broke down and I had to wait in the courthouse lock up for five hours after the trial stopped."

Leto opens his eyes and sits up in his bunk. "How'd the trial go?"

"My lawyer is calling people to the stand to testify on my behalf. I'm still screwed, but at least the testimony is more in my favor."

"Good for you. I confess. They put me in with you so I can get information that convicts you and puts you away for a long time. Don't worry man, I'm not a snitch

"Thanks Leto, I'd better turn in. I have another terrible headache. They're taking me back to the justice center early tomorrow."

"Good night."

"You too,"

I reached for my stash of brown sugar and popped half a pill, chased it with a drink of water. Laying in the darkness, I think of Maggie. Her memory sustains me. It seems like I've been dreaming of her every night since I arrived in this stinking dump. The dreams about Maggie have helped me more than anything.

I wasn't lying when I told Olivia that Maggie and I were only friends. As time passed, we began seeing more of each other. We enjoy each other's company. We had serious feelings for each other. Despite those feelings, I had reservations about her. She's been too perfect, too kind, and too considerate. I wish I trusted people more than I do.

. . . .

"This park was only two miles away from where I live. Who knew it even existed, much less that it was so close," said Maggie as she handed the corners of the blanket to me.

"A while back there was an article in the Sunday paper about this place being a U.S. Calvary Post way back when," I said. "Did you know the main trail at Homestead Park was part of a trail soldiers used to get up here? The hiking trail starts at my apartment complex."

"Oh, yeah. Have you hiked up here before?"

"Oh yeah, several times."

"So, Jack, do you want to continue holding the blanket and talk or should we spread it out on the grass?"

We spread the blanket out. Soon we were ready to enjoy a peaceful afternoon.

"Jack, are you okay? You seem a little preoccupied."

"I'm fine. Having this picnic brings back memories of my family. I can't remember the last time I went on a picnic. I think it was at Big Bear before the accident."

"What's Big Bear?"

"You're from LA and you've never heard of Big Bear Lake."

"I left LA when I was four years old and no, I never heard of Big Bear Lake."

"It's a lake high in the mountains east of Los Angeles. My mom and dad would take my sisters and I up to Big Bear camping in the summer. I have a lot of wonderful childhood memories with my sisters and my parents. We'd fish, go swimming and camp out in the woods. My dad told stories about a big hairy half man, half bear creature that roamed the woods during the night around the lake."

"No kidding?"

"What?"

"About the creature?"

"Maggie?"

"I'm serious."

I couldn't help but grin a little before responding. "My hunch is that my father made up the story."

"Yeah, I guess that's a little strange once you think about it." She removed her shoes and sat down on the blanket. She opened a blue cloth bag filled with different colored strings.

"What's that?"

"This?" Maggie pointed at her blue bag.

"Yeah."

"It's a blue bag full of strings. I thought I'd make you another friendship bracelet. I'll bet you didn't realize I was a professional friendship bracelet maker."

"Really?"

"No, not really," she answered with a snickered expression. "I learned how to make these at summer camp when I was a girl scout. Would you like a friendship bracelet?"

"I already have three of them... yeah, sure."

"What are your favorite two colors?"

"Green and Yellow."

"Cool. You realize if I make you a friendship bracelet, you can't ever take it off."

"Is that so?"

"Yes, it is so. Under penalty of law, if you remove the bracelet, you could be in trouble."

Maggie began making my green and yellow bracelet as I laid back and relaxed in the warm afternoon sunshine.

After fifteen minutes of silence, she looked at me and, out of the blue, asked, "Did you camp out in the woods with wild animals?"

"I'm sorry?"

"When you went up to that lake in LA."

"Are you talking about Big Bear Lake?"

"Yeah. Is that the place where you went camping with your mom and dad?"

"That's the place. Yes, we camped out in the woods. Do you want to know how many times wild animals attacked us in the middle of the night?"

"Not particularly."

"I'll tell you, anyway. Except for an occasional bat cruising over our head when we sat around the campfire, the wild beasts of the forest never bothered us. I can't believe you've never even heard of Big Bear?"

"I was born in LA but raised in Sacramento. My parents were not campers. They just weren't. I suspect they would rather have a root canal rather than go camping outside in the middle of nowhere."

"You don't know what you're missing. Didn't you say that your family lived in LA for a long time?"

"Oh yeah, I was born in Sherman Oaks. My mother's family started D'Angelo's Fine Dining restaurant in 1927 in downtown LA. My grandfather arrived from Poland because of anti-sematic fears."

"You're Jewish?"

"No. My grandfather was Jewish when he left Poland to work for his uncle's restaurant in Boston. It turns out his uncle was a lot more Jewish than my grandfather. In 1923, my grandfather got into an argument with his uncle and quit. With only fifteen dollars to his name, he worked his way across the country. All the way from Boston to Los Angeles, he met my grandmother in Henderson, Iowa. During his time in Iowa, he married and made enough money to complete his trip across the country. In April 1925 my grandparents arrived in LA. Three years later he opened D'Angelo's Fine Dining Restaurant."

"I thought your grandfather was Jewish. Why did he open an Italian Restaurant?"

"He was Jew-ish, and my grandmother was Baptist-ish. As for why they opened an Italian Restaurant, beats the hell out of me. During the holocaust, my grandfather's entire family vanished. My mother married Esperanzo Navarro, a line chef for my grandfather. My dad opened a restaurant in Sacramento. The rest is history."

"How did you end up here?"

"I met my husband, and this is where his practice is," answered Maggie. "I forgot are you from here?"

"No, my ex was born and raised here. She and our son left for Portland, Oregon, after our divorce."

I lay on my back to look up at the clouds sailing away in the warm afternoon breeze. Neither of us talked for the longest time when I leaned over and noticed Maggie, with green and yellow string on her belly, was sound asleep. I lay back and soon fell asleep myself. A crow began chattering at a squirrel, bringing us back to life.

Having a picnic was Maggie's idea. She prepared food and beverages. She brought along two folding chairs and an extra-large blanket to spread out so we could enjoy the afternoon. I couldn't stop thinking about Maggie's intent. What did she want? Our pseudo-relationship made no sense to me. First, she's married to a doctor with one of the largest practices in the city. I'm divorced. She was wealthy. I didn't know how wealthy she was, but I knew for sure it was a lot more money than I had. I could barely afford the apartment I've been renting. She was easy on the eye. I wasn't the handsomest dude on the block. What was she up to? I couldn't stop mulling over what was going on between her and me. I had to ask, "What's going on here, Maggie?"

"What do you mean?"

"Maggie, I enjoy your company, but we're complete opposites."

"I don't get what you're trying to say?"

"What would a woman like you see in a guy like me?"

"I enjoy your company. You're kind and I enjoy hanging out with you."

"I'm a project? A guy you can pity. Do I make you feel better when you're sitting around with your wealthy friends? Do you gloat about all the unfortunate little people you know?"

"Where the hell is that coming from? Is that what you think?"

"I'm not sure I know what to think about all this. I don't understand what you're up to."

"Remember awhile back when we had dinner at that little restaurant. Where that old lady waitress friend of yours threatened me."

"Olivia?"

"Yeah, your buddy Olivia threatened me. Is that what this is all about?"

"Oh, come on, give me a break. I told you that all she was trying to do was to protect me. Besides, she had nothing to do with what I've been thinking about. I just don't understand why an attractive, wealthy, married woman would want to be with me? If it's pity, I don't need or want it."

Maggie sat without speaking for a few minutes. "I don't know what to say. I enjoy your company. You seem to be a likeable guy." She sat for a few more uncomfortable minutes. "Yeah, I guess you were right. I just felt sorry for you. That's it." She sat up, turned toward me. "I think it's time we get going."

"Are you angry?"

"No, not at all. All I feel right now is pity." She gave me a fake smile. "Let's get going. I've got better things to do than sitting on this fucking hill."

"Maggie, I didn't mean to upset you, I just wanted to know what we're up to?"

"Well, I'm not up to a goddamn thing. Trust me, nothing," she stood up, grabbed the picnic basket and started walking toward her car. "Bring the blanket the folding chairs and hurry if you want a ride."

"Come on, Maggie. Let's at least talk about it."

"Don't forget the blanket."

I leaned down and grabbed the blanket in my arms. "It doesn't have to end this way. I don't understand why you're so pissed off."

"Let's go, I have better things to do today. I don't have time for your pity party."

"Why don't you leave without me, I'll walk back."

"Sounds like a great idea," answered Maggie as she tossed everything in the backseat. It seemed like seconds before she was on her way down the hill. I watched as she stuck her hand out of the window and flipped me the bird. It was surprising how quickly she had lost her temper, not to mention the intensity of her anger. I sat on one of the cement picnic tables and thought about what had just transpired. A few minutes passed before I began the hike down the trail to my apartment. Twenty minutes later when I approached my apartment, I saw her sitting on the staircase of my apartment building. She'd been crying. I wasn't sure what to expect. Was she going to yell at me again?

"Hey," I said so as not to surprise her.

"Hey Jack."

"Have you been here long?"

"I went back to look for you, but I couldn't find you. I'm sorry I got so upset."

"It wouldn't be the first time I pissed someone off and most likely won't be the last. Besides, I may have had a hand in what happened. Do you want to go to The Fourth Street Diner and grab some lunch? I'm hungry."

"I have all the food I made for lunch. Let's go in your apartment and have lunch there?"

"That's an even better idea. I'll get it."

"It's on the backseat of my car. How did the trial go for you today? I worry about you?"

"It's getting on my nerves. I don't understand why my trial keeps popping up in the middle of my dreams."

"I'm sorry, I wish there was something I could do to help you. It seems like I bear some responsibility for the mess you're in. I love you more than I've ever loved anyone in my life. Jack, please come away with me."

Chapter 16

Joe Hammer

S loan's Delicatessen is in the same building as the Marsh County District Attorney's office. The deli is on the first floor of the Cady Building. The DA's office is on the fifth floor.

I sat in the deli's corner reviewing the prosecution's so-called case against my client. I had an appointment with Jackson Maynard. My client made a positive impression on me. I believed Jack Holt was innocent. Regardless of my feelings about Jack, I had a conflicted mindset developed over the years of being a prosecutor.

Jackson Maynard broke my concentration when he stopped at my table. "Good morning, nice to see you again. It seems like old times. Are you getting a little homework done before our meeting?"

"Oh, hi Jackson. How are you? Please have a seat."

"I can't I need to get upstairs. Are you enjoying defending your client?"

"When I get him off your trumped-up charges, you'll have to eat a big pile of crow. Are you ready for our meeting?"

"I'm as ready as I'll ever be." Jackson looked at his watch. "I need to get going. See you in twenty minutes. Oh yeah Joe, before you venture upstairs you need to know something."

"What's that?"

"When people heard you were coming in for our meeting, they got a little antsy. The lawyers and support staff won't be greeting you with a lot of enthusiasm."

"Are you serious, Jackson? I would bet a month's pay that everyone up there worshiped me."

"One more thing, Detectives Nichols and Templeton will be at the meeting. They've yet to talk to your client and they're not happy campers. I'll see you in a few minutes."

He left the deli to go to his office on the fifth floor. A big swig of Pepto Bismol helped calm things down.

The fifth-floor offices of the Cady Building looked much the way it did when I worked for the DA. Margie, the receptionist, led me to a conference room where Jackson Maynard with the detectives were waiting.

"Good morning, guys," I took a deep breath, then sat down at the conference table. "It's been a while since we crossed paths. How are you?"

"Let's take a pass on the niceties," said Detective Nichols. "You don't give a damn how we're doing any more than we care about you. How about we talk about that creep you're defending?"

"Jerry, crawl out of your shell! I'm crushed. I just found out I was Mr. Holt's defense attorney two days ago. My predecessor, Mr. Rubio, only met him one time. In fairness to my client, you need to count to ten and take a deep breath."

"Screw you, Joe."

"Jerry," said Jackson, "tone it down." Turning to face me, "This is a frustrating case."

"No kidding? So, if Mr. Holt exercises his right not to speak to the police without counsel, that brings about suspicion."

"Yeah, in this case it did," answered Detective Templeton.

"I'm curious. What lead you to my client in the first place?"

"We wanted to find out what he knew about Maggie Stewart's murder," answered Detective Templeton.

"Come on, that's not an answer," I responded. "I read your police report. It said that Marilyn Pope had seen, and I quote. 'A creepy looking man lurking around the Stewart's home on the day Mrs. Stewart disappeared,' end quote. Did she say, lurking? Who uses that word anymore? Never mind. My question to you is how did you determine my client was someone who would help your case?"

"We went back to the crime scene where the girl scouts discovered the body of Mrs. Stewart. While double checking the area, we saw Mr. Holt walking on the main trail in Homestead Park," answered Detective Nichols.

"Okay?" I answered. "Did you question everyone who used the Main trail that afternoon?"

"What?" asked Detective Templeton.

"I don't understand. According to your police report a neighbor said she saw and I once again quote, 'A creepy looking man lurking around the Stewart's home on the day Mrs. Stewart disappeared,' end quote. My client was walking home from work. What was it about him in particular that made him a person of interest?"

Detective Templeton sat up in his chair. "Let me repeat this so you don't get confused. Mrs. Pope described a man with a facial disfigurement lurking around the Stewart's home on the day Maggie Stewart disappeared."

"If Mrs. Pope said that, then my question is, which one of you brainy guys didn't include those comments in the police report? You are the ones who might have screwed up. In the police report I received, it said Mrs. Pope said, and I quote. 'A creepy looking man lurking around the Stewart's home on the day Mrs. Stewart disappeared.' Which statement is correct? The statement you just said or the way it was in the police report?"

"It doesn't matter?" responded Detective Nichols.

"What do you mean it doesn't matter; it matters a hell of a lot to my client?"

"Okay, stop," said Jackson Maynard. "Joe, we have an autopsy report on Mrs. Stewart. I suspect you read the autopsy report."

"I did."

"Then you're aware the coroner found your client's semen in Mrs. Stewart's vagina."

"Okay?"

"How did your client's semen get inside Mrs. Stewart?" asked Jackson.

"Are you serious? Didn't your parents talk to you about the birds and the bees? It's obvious my client had sex with this woman. Grown-ups do that now and then."

"Okay," said Detective Nichols. "Are you implying it was consensual sex?"

"No, I not implying that at all. I'm saying it as a matter of fact that my client and Mrs. Stewart had sexual intercourse two times on the day she disappeared. It was consensual. It happens a lot, you know, like bunny rabbits. Come to think about it, maybe you don't know. Normal people do that stuff, especially young people. Do you want to know what I think?"

"Sure," answered Jackson.

"I think these two detectives got pissed off because they had no clue who may have murdered Mrs. Stewart. Then, by coincidence, my client just walked by as he does every day on his way home from work. You assumed that Mr. Holt's facial features were equal to a creepy-looking guy. I suspect you assumed his guilt as soon as you saw him. An assumption based on my client's facial disfigurement. It's not what you said in your report, but what you didn't say in your police report. Isn't that correct?"

"Enlighten us Joe," asked Jackson.

"The only reference to Mr. Holt's facial features is this woman's statement about seeing, and I quote. 'A creepy looking man lurking around the Stewart's home on the day Mrs. Stewart disappeared,' end of quote. Why my client? It seems to me there might have been other directions you might have taken other than taking the simple route and focusing on my client. I realize you want to speak with my client. Here's a heads-up. I'm moving to exclude everything you discovered because of an executed search warrant. These clowns didn't have valid grounds for probable cause. As soon as the judge rules in our favor, I'll ask her to rule on a motion to dismiss. That way we all don't have to go to court. That way we've saved the county a lot of money prosecuting a case that should never go to court. Let's just say you guys screwed up chasing what you consider low hanging fruit. The best thing for you to do is to cut your losses and move on to real criminals."

"I see two years off haven't changed you a bit. Before your last statement, I was considering offering him a plea bargain just to show you I'm not a heartless bastard! I should have known better. You don't have a chance in hell that Judge Taylor will rule in your favor," said Jackson. "The fact is that you're wasting everyone's time and money."

"Wow guys," I answered. "It looks like you have me in a corner. Here's something to consider. Your police report shows photos of my client's body from the waist up. I looked at those photos and saw nothing except a few scars from an automobile accident he was in as a kid and a few freckles. Did you, by any chance, notice in the photos of my client's upper torso that his left arm is smaller than his right arm. It's called atrophy. That alone means it is impossible for my client to have choked Maggie Stewart to death."

"If he has nothing to hide, then why did he refuse to talk to us?" asked Detective Nichols.

"He doesn't trust police officers, especially detectives," I responded. "If you want to interrogate my client, I'd be happy to set that up. I've already have a meeting scheduled with him at one tomorrow afternoon. If you'd like, I'll let you talk to my client under my supervision," I said, turning to Jackson. "Read your own police and autopsy report before you pursue this prosecution further. Speaking as a former prosecutor, this is a classic case of detectives not doing their job. In the spirit of cooperation, can you be at the county detention center at two tomorrow afternoon?"

"Trust me, we'll be there at two o'clock sharp," answered Detective Nichols.

"Good, I'm looking forward to it," I answered. "Why don't you explain to me why you didn't include the search warrant in your police report?"

"I thought you said you'd read the report?" asked Detective Templeton.

"I did," I answered. "I read all about what you discovered. How you got the DNA sample from his toothbrush."

"I see you're the same old pain in the ass you've always been," answered Detective Nichols.

"You could be right, detective. And both of you are lazy rookies detectives who didn't do their jobs. Now that we've establish that we're three guys with shitty personalities, can we move on? Accusing me of being obnoxious jerk that nobody likes is getting old. Just for the hell of it, where's the probable cause? What information was used to get a search warrant in the first place?"

Chapter 17

Jack Holt

"I met Jackson Maynard, the prosecuting attorney. The two detectives who took you into custody were there."

"Oh, yeah," responded Jack.

"They're convinced that you're guilty. I read the police report against you. I asked them what else they had because it looked to me like they were hedging their entire case on one premise."

"What's that?"

"They based their entire case on the assumption you were obsessed with Maggie Stewart. They claim you started stocking her, and then you raped her. To cover your tracks, you murdered her and buried her in the park."

"Gee, what a surprise."

"The prosecution is going after your character. Just so you know, the prosecution might bring your ex-wife in as a witness."

"Why would they bring her in? We haven't talked in years."

"Let's talk about your marriage. Do you remember I said that we have to be honest and trust each other?"

"Yeah."

"Well, I hate surprises. You don't know me from the man in the moon. Please believe me when I tell you I will give this everything I've got. To do justice for you, I have to know everything. What happened with your marriage?"

"I screwed it up. We were young, and she did nothing wrong. It was one hundred percent my fault."

"Were you charged with two DUIs and a domestic violence charge?"

"Yeah, but not really. I'm not proud of that period of my life. I didn't understand how she could love me considering the way I look. We were having financial problems because I was having a hard time finding and keeping a job. The pressure mounted when she became pregnant. It got worse after our son Jake was born. I came into our marriage with a lot of baggage because of my face. I drank too much and what can I say?"

"What about the domestic violence charge?"

"That's not true. The police officers took me in, but they filed no charges against me. I've never hit my wife. On the night they took me into custody, my wife and I had a big fight after I came home drunk. A neighbor called the police because I was being too loud. Before I got home, my wife fell down as she walked home. The fall caused a black eye and bruises on her face and arms. When the police officers arrived, they saw the bruises on my wife's face and handcuffed me. I was drunk and insisted that I didn't hit my wife. She told them the same thing, but it looked like she was covering for me. They took me into custody and let me go the next day. Like I said, they filed no charges. I did a lot of stupid things, but I've never abused my wife or anyone else."

"You didn't hit your wife then or ever?"

"That's right. I've never been violent with her or anyone."

"Do you have a relationship with your son?"

"No, I've stayed away from my ex and my son."

"Why?"

"I caused both of them too much grief. They are much better off."

"Do you not want a relationship with your son?"

"In a perfect world, of course. Under the circumstances, all I can offer is to let them be. I've caused them enough pain."

"Did the court order you to pay child support?"

"Yes, but I never paid a single support payment."

"This could hurt your case; it shows your lack of character. Why didn't you pay your child support?"

"I had a hard time getting and keeping a job."

"If I were the prosecutor, I'd focus on that aspect of your behavior. I know Jackson Maynard. Trust me, he will focus on the way you treated your ex-wife. He will say you're a little unhinged."

"Yeah, I figured as much. I did what I did and I'm not proud of it. All I can say is that since I got divorced, I've grown up."

"Here's what I worry about. You said you had consensual sex with Mrs. Stewart. The prosecution will use that against you for several reasons. First, the prosecutor will ask you, why would she have sex with you? After you answer the question, he will reframe the circumstances to discredit your answer. He'll say Mrs. Stewart was a world-famous model worth millions, married to a successful respected doctor. He'll finish by pointing out that you've had three jobs in the past five years. Police charged you with two DUIs. They also took you in on suspicion of domestic violence. You haven't paid a nickel in child support. What the hell, Jack! Why on Earth would Maggie Stewart have anything to do with you?"

"I understand. Our relationship took a year and a half to develop. Believe me, I wondered what she saw in me. I told her everything about my past. I didn't hide or try to spin anything about myself."

"Why would a married woman start a relationship with you?"

"Maggie's marriage was on paper only. Her husband is a super control freak, not to mention a real creep. He wanted her at home and was jealous when others paid any attention to her. He insisted that everything in the cupboards be a certain way. That included the food in the pantry. That everything had to be in straight rows, or he'd go off the deep end. The same was true for the refrigerator. She told me that her husband would put labels on his food in the refrigerator to make sure she wouldn't eat any of his food. Isn't that the weirdest thing you've ever heard?"

I stopped talking and stared at Jack's face. After a long, hard, uncomfortable look, I understood without a doubt that Jack Holt was innocent. I worried the prosecution's case would be enough to convict him of first-degree sexual assault and murder. Juror prejudice alone could put my client in prison for life. I remembered prosecuting people myself for looking like they did the crime. It was no accident that at the trial the jury came to a guilty conclusion based on appearance alone. As a prosecutor, I used the jury's bigotry to get convictions and further my career. All I had to do to persuade the twelve bigoted jurors was to imply guilt based on looks alone. Using evidence that was circumstantial and questionable assured a conviction. I felt a knot in the pit of my stomach. I reached into my coat pocket, took out a small bottle of Pepto Bismol, and took a drink, wiping the pink from my lips. Everything I did as a prosecutor was within the law and the rules of evidence. That leaves a gigantic area within the law to protect ourselves.

"I've heard everything at least a dozen times. Believe me, nothing is surprising. Let's talk about your relationship with Maggie Stewart. When your relationship began, what did she see in you? Jack, you know this much better than I do, but your face is on trial. No one on the prosecution's team will admit it. Their case revolves around the question: would a woman like Maggie Stewart have an intimate relationship with a guy who looks like you. The prosecution's case focused on your facial features. They'll do it by innuendo. Trust me, they will play on the jury's bigotry and fears. A neighbor told police she saw, 'a creepy-looking guy lurking around the Stewart's home on the day Mrs. Stewart disappeared.' Her words, not mine. When the detectives noticed you in the park, you became the focus of their attention. You became the ghoulish drooling creep who plotted, raped, and then murdered a beautiful innocent unsuspecting woman. This is a classic Hollywood murder story. You are after all the quintessential movie bad guy. When you refused to talk to the detectives without legal counsel, you kind of screwed yourself. I understand why you did it, but it didn't help your case. In your defense, you were most likely screwed no matter what you did. The detectives and Jackson Maynard are lazy. They're bureaucrats who are working hard to make their careers look as promising as possible. Trust me to some people in the DA's office. The office politics and career objectives take priority over justice every day of the week. You're nothing but another trophy case in their personnel file of conquests. I don't know how they got a search warrant to search your apartment. Yesterday afternoon I moved to exclude. The evidence police discovered resulted from the illegal search warrant. If Judge Taylor agrees, the prosecution has no case."

"Oh yeah? Do you think she will exclude everything?"

"No, but it will throw the prosecutors off their strategy. It will put the subject of your facial features front and center. The odds are not in our favor," I answered. "We have to give it a shot."

"I understand."

"Explain to me what Maggie Stewart saw in you?"

Jack told me about their relationship. He also talked about Maggie's plans to divorce her husband. She financed the building and the equipment for his successful medical practice. All she wanted was a clean divorce and to end her terrible marriage with him once and for all. Maggie hired a lawyer to help her put a strategy together to dissolve their marriage. Jack couldn't remember the lawyer's name. Jack and Maggie checked her out on the Internet, and she seemed to be just what Maggie was looking for. All Jack could remember was that she had a reputation for being a lawyer who played to win. She had a reputation for doing her homework, then going for the opposition's throat. The only ruthless bitch female divorce lawyer that came to my mind was Penelope Bergdorf. The instant I mentioned her name; it all came back. Yes, Penelope Bergdorf was the lawyer who represented Maggie.

"Are you kidding me? Do you know her?"

'Ah hell,' I thought to myself as I went into a panic. I swear, that woman is like a bad coin, she keeps coming back into my life. What are the odds?

"Are you okay?"

"Yeah, I'm okay. Unfortunately, you're not the only one with a checkered past. I've known her for many years. She was my wife's divorce lawyer. That damn woman took me for every penny I had."

"I'm sorry."

"You know how you told me that your divorce was all your fault?"

"Yeah."

"The same thing happened to me. I had it coming when I went through my divorce. That's a different story. Sorry for getting off track."

"Was it another example of you being an asshole?"

"Pretty much. I have to admit Penelope was feisty as hell. She works with a retired detective named David Sinclair. I knew David when he was a city cop. At the time we had a friendly working relationship. The relationship ended when he used his skills to screw me during my divorce. Like I said, I brought all this on myself."

The detectives arrived for their first interrogation of my client. Following my instructions, Jack plead the fifth on about half the questions. Even after the detectives finished, their anger towards my client remained, and their rage towards me intensified.

· · · ·

At four-thirty that afternoon, Jackson Maynard and I met with Judge Diane Taylor in her chambers.

"Good afternoon," said the judge. "And welcome back, Joe. We have two objectives for our meeting this afternoon. The first is to talk about Joe's motion to exclude. I have another motion to dismiss should I agree with the defense counsel. If I do that Jackson, your case is dead in the water. Do you have any other evidence against Mr. Holt?"

"That is the core of our case, your Honor."

"I read your motion," said the judge. "Tell me what your problem is with the prosecution's case?"

"Detectives focused in on Mr. Holt because a neighbor saw, 'a creepy-looking guy lurking around the Stewart's home,' their words not mine. Based on that statement, the detectives began focusing on my client's facial features. On the assumption that the words, 'creepy looking guy,' the detectives singled out my client. At the time they assumed Mr. Holt was guilty, they did not have any evidence about the crime. I've yet to see any probable cause that would merit a search warrant. They based the warrant on a woman identifying Mr. Holt after seeing a photo taken by the detectives. The essence of my motion is to exclude anything police found because of this unfounded search warrant."

"How about you, Jackson?" asked the judge.

"I don't like the words the neighbor used to describe Mr. Holt. They are in fact demeaning, not to mention insulting. It's not right, but in our culture, people assume that someone who has a facial difference is creepy or disturbed. You don't have to go any further than our movies or our literature to find disfigured people portrayed as the antagonist in a story. My detectives deny any prejudice regarding Mr. Holt's facial differences. In all honesty, they may have become suspicious because of Mr. Holt's facial features. When Stewart's neighbor identified Mr. Holt, the detectives, as any reasonable detective would, followed the lead. When the detectives went to talk to Mr. Holt, he refused to talk to them. I understand he has every right not to talk to detectives, but as we all know, that only increased their suspicion of Mr. Holt."

"Your honor," I asked, "may I mention a point of concern when I read the police report?"

"Go ahead, Joe," answered the judge.

"I couldn't help but notice that Eric Warren may have played a part with the decision to focus on my client."

"Do you know this for a fact?" asked the judge.

"Your Honor, it's an assumption based on some missing statements in the police report. An assumption based on an odd omission from the police report I downloaded," answered Joe.

"Why didn't you bring this up this morning?" asked Jackson.

"Because my client didn't want to talk to the detectives. Jackson, there's a valid reason for a lack of confidence in many police forces."

The judge looked at each lawyer, thinking about her next move. "Joe, I understand why you submitted your motion to exclude, but I'm denying your motion. I have no opinion about any behind-the-scenes politics of this case. If you find any evidence, please bring it to my attention. I would suggest you talk to each other. Let's move on to setting a court date. I'm thinking April twenty-eighth would be a suitable date for me. How about you?"

April twenty-eighth gave Joe six weeks to get up to speed with his client and the circumstances of Maggie Stewart's murder.

"Okay, I think we're done here," said Judge Taylor. "Jackson, if you don't mind, I'd like to talk to Joe about something not related to the case."

"No problem," answered Jackson as he turned toward me. "Maybe we can get together to talk about things."

"Sure, I'll call you tomorrow and we'll set things up."

"Sounds good," answered Jackson. "Thank you, Your Honor."

"Have a nice evening, Jackson," said the judge.

• • • •

"How are you, Joe?"

"I'm fine, I'm glad to be back in the game."

"That's what I wanted to talk to you about."

Thinking the judge was about to give me yet another lecture about my less than desirable personality.

"I'm trying to figure out why Judge Horton became your champion and allowed you to practice law again?"

"Yeah, I understand, I wish I could tell you, Your Honor. I'm as puzzled as you are. A few weeks ago, I was mixing paint at Hector's Home Improvement."

"I understand you're on probation and you have only one client. Is that right?"

"Yes."

"What makes Jack Holt so important?"

"I can't answer that, Your Honor, I'm not being coy. I don't know why Judge Horton gave me this case."

"Are you okay?"

"Yeah, I'm a little rusty, but I'm doing the best I can to help my client."

"Your client is one lucky man to have a lawyer of your caliber representing him. There is one thing I have to ask you. I spoke with your boss, Jackie. We're long-time personal friends. You impressed Jackie. I hope your days of being a jackass are over. I'd rather not see the old Joe in my courtroom. Is that going to be a problem?"

"I will defend my client to the best of my abilities. We may have our legal arguments, but the old Joe is gone for good."

"Welcome back."

Chapter 18

1 :35 PM-Wednesday, Day Two
There are too many power plays being made during deliberations. Some on the jury don't seem to care much about the purpose of the trial. A man's life is hanging in the balance. It seems like those who speak up have to put up with insults. Many of the jurors are so frustrated that they seem to have dropped out of the deliberations altogether. We are stuck in a situation that seems hopeless. The message was loud and clear from Henry: He either gets what he wants, or he'll hang the jury, end of subject. I will continue trying to get everyone to work together.

• • • •

"By a show of hands, how many of you agree to review each person who gave testimony during the trial?" asked the foreperson. She watched as all the jurors raised their hands in agreement. "Great. How many of you agree that we'll start in the order the witnesses appeared on the witness stand? We'll start with the prosecution witnesses in the order they appeared during the proceedings. Afterwards, we'll go through the witnesses for the defense. With a show of hands, how many agree to proceed the way I just described?" I watched as each juror raised his or her hand in agreement. Everyone agreed. "Then I suggest we get going. Does anyone have anything to say about Doctor Daniel Stewart?"

"Before we begin, I want to change my vote from guilty to not guilty," said Hassan Saragana while staring at Henry Keller.

"I also want to change my vote to not guilty," said Marty Chu.

"Okay," said the foreperson, "I believe we are at six to six."

"Does anyone else have anything to say before we get into the testimony?" asked the foreperson. Everyone was quiet. "Okay, who wants to start with Doctor Stewart?"

"I'll be glad to start if no one minds," said Juror Number 2, Sara King. "I most likely wouldn't have noticed had I been sitting further away from the witness stand. There he sat, no further than three or four feet in front of me. I believed everything that doctor had said until he cried. I noticed he was putting us on because his eyes were as dry as a bone. When I was a child, and I didn't get my way, I'd start pretending to cry. My mother looking me straight in the eyes would say, Child if you ain't well'n up they ain't crying so you'd better knock it off or for damn sure I'll give you something to cry about."

"That is so interesting. I thought the same thing for different reasons," said Marty Chu. "I was sitting in the back row next to the audience, the furthest from the witness stand. During his testimony, when the doctor started talking about his wife, he got emotional and cried. When he got emotional, I questioned his sincerity. I couldn't put my finger on why I felt that way. As I listened to Sara, I realized no one offered the doctor a tissue. When people are around someone who cries, it's a natural thing to get them a tissue. I mean, who doesn't do that? Thanks to Sara, the reason no one offered him a tissue is that he wasn't crying. Sara is right, that guy was bullshitting everyone in the courtroom. To me, there's more to him than he lets on."

"I have to admit, I didn't get that impression at all. I seldom tear up when I cry," said Linda.

Kayla mumbled under her breath as she shook her head. "Are you afraid your tears would freeze?"

Linda ignored Kayla and talked to the jury. "I don't have a clue what Sara and Marty are implying. Did either of you listen to his credentials? Why would he lie about his wife's murder? There's no reason at all. It doesn't even make sense."

"Are you serious? What do the doctor's medical credentials have to do with this trial? I can't figure out why you would even make such a statement," said Kayla. Michael Eckert addressed his response to Linda. "I'll try to answer your question. Why did they go over the doctor's credentials? It had to do with the trial. The answer is nothing. When the defense lawyer tried to ask the doctor about a case where police charged him with drugging and raping a high school girl. The prosecutor objected; the judge agreed. When the defense lawyer tried to ask the doctor about other stories, questioning his credibility, the same thing happened. Whatever the stories were, the prosecutor got so worked up. The prosecutor's actions say a lot about the doctor's credibility. Does everyone remember the defense's last question? He asked the doctor if he was right, or left-handed? Why would he do that? Am I the only one who remembers that?"

All the jurors remember the defense lawyer asking the doctor if he was right- or left-handed. The doctor answered that he was left-handed.

"Let me remind everybody," said Henry Keller. "We're obliged to base our opinions on facts, not this nonsense about what you think may have happened. When the judge ordered us to ignore what a few of the witnesses said, we're obligated to obey her orders."

"That sounds great, but we can't ignore what took place in front of our own eyes," said Michael Eckert, sitting on the right side of the foreperson. "I got the impression the judge got annoyed with the defense lawyer. I didn't know what was going on between the two, but it wasn't good. Even the prosecutor was playing them to his favor. How are we supposed to ignore all this stuff?"

"Well," responded Henry. "All I'm saying is that we can't just make up our own theories about the case, we're deliberating. We have to base our decision on the facts alone."

"It was obvious to all of us that the judge got annoyed by the defense lawyer. That affected what we heard about the case and the defendant," said Michael Eckert as he looked at the other jurors, then focused on Henry Keller. "Henry, I have to say something to you. As most of you I suppose have already surmised, I'm kind of easygoing, let it slide kind of guy. Henry, you need to know you don't intimidate me one damn bit. If you're smart, you'll watch what's coming out of your mouth. I don't know what your problem is, but you need to add to the conversation and stop attacking other jurors."

"Please stop," interrupted the foreperson. "Let's all take a deep breath. Okay? How many times do I have to say this? We will not make progress if we keep being rude to each other. I realize we're all frustrated, but this behavior isn't helping. I have my own concerns about parts of the doctor's testimony, if you'll be kind enough to let me explain. My grandfather was a country doctor who made house calls in rural Chiricahua County, Arizona. Papa was the sweetest old man who was always working either in his office or out in the countryside, seeing patients. He didn't have a clue what my grandmother did around the house. His participation in raising my mother and my uncle when they were kids was minimal. Here's my point, Doctor Stewart has the largest gastroenterology practice in town. He has two doctors/partners and a staff of eleven nurses and support people. He's busier than my grandfather ever thought about being. When the defense lawyer cross-examined the doctor, he listed everything his wife was 'chartered' to do. It took me back when the doctor used the word 'chartered'. What was that about? Who uses that word when referring to any family member, much less his own wife? Did he think of her as a hired hand? I don't know about you, but my husband is a nurse like me, and he couldn't tell anyone how things get done around the house. Does anyone else think it's odd that Dr. Stewart knows so much about what his wife did around the house?"

"In our apartment," responded Kayla. "My husband doesn't know diddley squat. We both work full-time jobs, and I love my husband with all my heart. The fact is, he doesn't have a clue where anything is or how things get done around our apartment. It's stunning what my husband chooses not to know."

· · · ·

O ver the next hour, we all shared what we were thinking about and ideas about aspects of the doctor's testimony. There was no agreement about the doctor other than none of us, even those who defended him, aren't rushing off to be his patient.

The next witness for the prosecution was the Stewart's neighbor, Marilyn Pope. The defense lawyer asked her to read the sentence that the prosecution's case centered on. "A creepy looking man lurking around the Stewart's house on the day Mrs. Stewart disappeared." She was nervous about testifying in a courtroom. At one time, the judge asked her if she was okay. She said she'd be fine. Her testimony was straightforward and lasted less than twenty minutes. What made her testimony noteworthy was her use of the term 'creepy looking man.' Upon further testimony, she made a confusing remark when she said to her way of thinking there was nothing negative or insulting to the phrase, 'A creepy-looking man.'

At one point, the lawyer for the defense showed a photograph of Jack Holt. He asked Mrs. Pope if she could describe Mr. Holt from the photograph. Did you tell the detectives you saw a 'creepy looking man lurking around the Stewart's home on the day Mrs. Stewart disappeared?' When she verified the photograph, she said the exact words. The defense thanked her and told the judge he had no more questions.

The jury moved on to Jerry Nichols, one of the two homicide detectives who investigated the murder. He mentioned that Mrs. Pope saw, "a creepy-looking man lurking around the Stewart's home on the day Mrs. Stewart disappeared." He noted her statement by saying it was Mrs. Pope's words, not his description. During Detective Nichols's testimony, the defense focused on why the detectives focused on his client.

"That's the trouble with America," said Henry Keller. "We've become too politically correct. It doesn't matter what words someone uses to describe Mr. Holt's appearance. The fact is whether it was superb detective skills or just plain luck they got the right man. They took him off the street before he could hurt other innocent women. It's a damn slippery slope if we question the motives of our men and women on the police force."

"Excuse me?" said Oscar Rosenthal. "Sir, you are one of the most offensive people I've ever met, and I've met many people in my lifetime. We have a right and a responsibility to question all forms of power no matter if they are politicians, soldiers, police, doctors, or lawyers. The vast majority of these people understand and take their responsibilities seriously. These people want to make things better for as many people as possible. Unfortunately, some professionals fall victim to their frailties. Just because someone is a police officer, a doctor, or a lawyer doesn't mean they are above scrutiny. Sir, need I remind you that accountability comes with the job."

"You must admit, there are too many people questioning the people who protect this country and our freedoms," said Henry, his face flushed with anger as he paces the jury room. "The media, the bloggers, and every Tom, Dick, and Harry who has an opinion. Ninety percent of it is fake news with a liberal agenda. We should shut down the liberal media. I want to be on the record with everyone. That son-of-a bitch is guilty as hell, and if I had my way, I'd execute the faggot myself. He's a goddamn disgrace. I wish he was dead."

"Henry, are you okay?" asked the foreperson. "What's going on? I don't know how to respond and you're scaring everyone."

"I'm fine," Henry said, sitting down and taking a drink of water.

"Henry," said the foreperson/nurse, "how about we all take fifteen minutes?"

"I'm fine," answered Henry.

"Okay, Mr. Rosenthal, you can finish your thought."

"I'm glad we have a system of checks and balances. Everyone on this jury should understand that. The fundamentals of our government are the rule of law and a system of checks and balances. Truth to power is our foundation. Look at our history. The founders designed our government for citizens to scrutinize. It's the sacred obligation of every citizen to question those in power. If all you will do is wave the flag and thump the bible you aren't a dutiful citizen, you're being manipulated to accomplish another person's agenda."

"Mr. Rosenthal," said Ira McMillian. "Do you think the defense lawyer may have gone a little overboard in his quest to discredit Detective Nichols? I mean, he wouldn't stop until the judge threatened him."

Oscar thought for a few seconds before answering. "I believe the prosecutor and the judge kept us from hearing something. The defense grilled the witness with how a judge approved the search warrant. The prosecutor became angry at the questioning by the defense of Detective Nichols. We will most likely never understand."

I remember the prosecution called Detective Templeton to back up Detective Nichols's testimony. The defense had no questions for Detective Templeton.

We moved on to the coroner's testimony. The prosecution called Dr. Khalid Shah, the Marsh County Coroner, to testify about his findings about Maggie Stewart's autopsy. The foreperson felt the coroner's testimony was so important that she requested a copy of the transcript. She read the coroner's responses when being cross-examined by the lawyer for the defense to the jury.

• • • •

"Dr. Shah," the defense lawyer began. "During the autopsy, did you determine the cause of death?"

"Yes."

"What caused Mrs. Stewart's death?"

"Strangulation."

"Could you explain what that is?"

"Strangulation is compressing the airway by using hands or some kind rope or cable."

"Doctor Shah, based on your findings, did Maggie Stewart have sexual intercourse before her death?"

"Yes."

"For the jury's sake, what made you come to that conclusion?"

"I found semen inside Mrs. Stewart's vagina."

"From that you determined she had sexual intercourse?"

"Yes. The semen proves without a doubt that Mrs. Stewart had intercourse within two hours of her death."

"Were there any signs of violence associated with Mrs. Stewart's death?"

"The only signs of violence against Mrs. Stewart were to the right side of her face and strangulation around her throat."

"Could those signs be evidence that she was in fact assaulted?"

"Yes, there is a slight possibility, but there were no signs of violence against Mrs. Stewart. She had no bruises in and around her genitalia. There was no bruising on her arms and nothing under her fingernails indicative of a violent act."

"What did you discover?"

In cases of assault, investigators only come across semen in women.

"Was Mrs. Stewart assaulted?"

"I would answer that question in this manner. There is a ninety-five percent chance that Mrs. Stewart had voluntary sexual intercourse hours before her death. I did not find any evidence of sexual assault."

"You testify that Mrs. Stewart's cause of death was strangulation. Is that correct?"

"Yes."

"How did you determine the cause of death was strangulation?"

"There was significant bruising on her neck and trachea. In fact, her assailant crushed her trachea by two opposing thumbs strong enough to block her air way resulting in her death."

"For the jury's benefit, I would like to revisit some of your testimony. Could you summarize the autopsy of Mrs. Stewart?"

"The murderer struck Mrs. Stewart on the right side of her face. He used his left hand made into a fist hit her with such force that it no doubt knocked her unconscious. Based on the wounds, the assailant then strangled her to death."

"How do you know the attacker hit her with his left hand made into a fist?"

"I assumed the attacker was facing her. The injury to the right side of her mandible and cheekbone was significant. Not enough to cause death, but enough to knock her unconscious."

"Do you know for a fact she was unconscious?"

"No. I came to that conclusion because there were no visible signs of a struggle."

"Could you conclude her attacker is left-handed since the blow to her face was on her right side?"

"Yes. The attacker was left-handed or ambidextrous."

"How certain are you of that?"

"I'd say ninety-nine percent sure."

"I want to make sure I understand your testimony."

"How was Mrs. Stewart strangled?"

"The attacker used both hands around her neck to strangle her."

"Did you determine that for a fact?"

"Yes. It is a statement of fact. Mrs. Stewart's death resulted from strangulation. Someone with two powerful hands caused her death."

"You testify there was semen found in Mrs. Stewart. Is that correct?"

"Yes."

"For the jury's sake, did you determine whose semen it was?"

"Yes. After doing a DNA test on the semen found in her body and a sample of Mr. Holt's saliva from his apartment. It was an exact DNA match."

"How did you get a sample of Mr. Holt's saliva?"

"Detective Nichols supplied the sample. I believe it was from Mr. Holt's apartment. The semen in Mrs. Stewart's body came from the defendant, Jack Holt."

"Were there any signs anywhere that a sexual assault took place?"

"No."

"And you checked her entire body?"

"Yes, I did. I checked under her fingernails, her hands, her arms, her entire vaginal area, her anus, and abdomen. There were no signs of struggle."

"Doctor Shah, you are a medical doctor?"

"Yes."

"If a man had significant muscle atrophy on, let's say his left arm and hand, would he have the strength in that arm to choke a person to death?"

"It depends."

"What do you mean, it depends?"

"It depends on how severe the muscle atrophy is."

"Have you looked at Jack Holt's medical records?"

"Yes."

"Doctor Shah, does my client have the muscle strength to choke someone to death?"

"I'm not qualified to answer that question, however I doubt a person with muscle atrophy would have the strength to kill an adult."

"Your Honor I object to this line of questioning," said the prosecutor.

"I'll withdraw the questions about my clients atrophy," turning to Dr. Shah, "Thank you, Dr. Shah. I'm finished with this witness."

· · · ·

The foreperson put down the transcripts. "I have to tell you; I'm becoming more confident that the defendant is innocent. Does anyone else have the same concerns I do?"

"Yeah, I do," Mike Shepard replied. "When we started there was no doubt in my mind the defendant was guilty. I'm kind of disappointed in myself that I missed these apparent details. I don't want to send an innocent man to prison any more than I want to let a cold-blooded murderer go free. There has to be justice regarding Jack Holt. Now I understand when they say justice is blind. It's a lot easier to decide when I have no personal stake in the game."

· · · ·

We discussed the coroner's testimony for another hour. Mike Shepard changed his vote to innocent. No one else changed their opinion about the defendant's guilt. We continued talking about the next two witnesses the prosecution called. The last two witnesses for the prosecution were there to impugn Jack Holt's credibility. A former female coworker filed a complaint of sexual harassment against Jack Holt. The complaint had no merit. Police dropped the charges. By planting a seed with the jury, the prosecution intended to establish that the defendant had a history of sexual misconduct toward women.

Jack had his car repaired at a mechanic, who was the other witness. During the testimony, the mechanic attested that Jack Holt had informed him the damage to his face resulted from combat.

Although the lawyer for the defense dispelled both witnesses, it was in the trial record.

Chapter 19

Jack Holt

"Where's Leto?" I asked anyone who might hear my voice. "That fat ass night guard came and got him about an hour ago," answered the inmate from somewhere in the darkness of the next cell block. "I think he's having a meeting with his lawyer."

"Is everything okay?" I asked.

"I don't know. He seemed fine to me. You're getting in late tonight."

"Yeah, the shuttle driver was late again."

"Can I ask you something?"

"Yeah, what's up?"

"I hear you and Leto talking about your trial for the past five nights. Do you think you will beat the rap?"

"I doubt it. I guess I'll be spending the rest of my life in prison."

"Do you like that Joe Hammer guy?"

"Yeah, he's okay. I think he's doing the best he can."

"He was the prosecutor when I went to prison the first time. My lawyer hates him."

"Yeah, he told me he was an Assistant County Attorney for most of his career."

"How did your trial go today?"

"My ex-wife testified today."

"That doesn't sound good."

"My lawyer suggested we use her for a defense witness. How could my ex to testify on my behalf. I treated her like shit, and I haven't seen my son in fourteen years. My lawyer told me to trust him. She said some things that I rather she didn't but overall, she was sweet."

"Not my ex-wife, she would crucify me if she had the chance."

"Hey, nothing personal, but I'm tired as hell. I want to hit the sack."

"That's cool."

I grabbed my stash of brown sugar and took half of a pill. All my troubles melted away as I drifted off to sleep.

. . . .

Our bodies lay beneath the warm cocoon of the sheets and blankets. Maggie and I had been laying in my bed lost in our thoughts, questioning what just happened and where our relationship was going?

"I'm sorry for getting you upset," I said as I rolled over to check the time. "In case you hadn't noticed, I can get cynical from time to time. I don't think of myself as a jackass. I've never have been a pretty boy and never will be. My temperament plus a shitload of other baggage cost me my first marriage. I'm always questioning people's motives, especially those who appear kind to me. That's why I asked you what was going on between us. Most people are uncomfortable around me. I've learned to be skeptical of most people. Sometimes I can't help but wonder why a person like you would be interested in me. It makes little sense. You are everything I'm not."

"Jack, there's no need to apologize, I get why you asked me. You had every right to question my motives. At first, all I wanted to do was to thank you for being so kind to me that morning in the park. You were so sweet; I'll never forget that gesture. When we met in the grocery store, I must admit I felt sorry for you. I know, I sound like a pretentious bitch, but that's the truth. To be honest with you, there is a part of me that feels uncomfortable around you. I feel awkward talking about your looks because I don't want to hurt your feelings. Remember when I asked you if you'd like to have dinner with me."

"Sure."

Maggie laid on her back, thinking about how to say what was on her mind.

"Maggie, just say it. If you have something to say, just say what's on your mind."

"When I asked you out that night, I was being a selfish bitch. I wanted to thank you for being kind to me, so I asked you out to give you the privilege of going out with someone who is as beautiful as me. Goddamn, that sounds so awful. I thought you'd choose an expensive, classy restaurant, but you chose the little cafe instead. Between the ambience of the old building, the amazing food plus watching how the old waitress fussed over you changed me. Olivia thought I was up to no good, and in a way she was right. What happened that evening is I began having genuine feelings for you. Now I have to admit I think about you all the time. You have been in my dreams since I was a little girl. Us falling in love was the best thing that ever happened to me. I never want to lose you; you're not another awful decision. Trust me, I know you're the guy, I just know."

"I don't know what to say," I answered. "I fell in love with the way you are, not how you look. Although I have to admit you are easy on the eye. I know you had nothing to do with it, but what the hell. That old man at Reggie's who keeps staring at your ass has excellent taste. This is just a wild ass guess, but I'm thinking we could have a bit of an issue with your husband."

"Yeah, I know I married a control freak that steps out on me all the damn time. He only married me because I have a lot of money. I'm hiring a divorce lawyer," said Maggie as she rolled over, facing me nose to nose. She touched the paralyzed side of my face, then gave me a kiss. "I haven't had the best luck with men. I'm so lucky that I met you. You are the best thing to happen to me."

"Are you okay?"

"Every time I'm with you, I'm okay. Other than my father and my brother, you're the first man I've met that I feel safe with. I've not told anyone this and you won't believe how many men have tried to have sex with me. A multi-millionaire, two famous television bible thumping preachers, a congressman, a Senator, movie stars, plus many other men have felt me up or tried to. One time, my fat ass agent wanted to meet me in his hotel room for a so-called meeting in his Paris hotel. When I arrived, he answered the door wearing a bathrobe. As soon as he closed the door, he removed his bathrobe. He was naked and had an erection. It terrified me. He guided me throughout my entire career. There were rumors, but I ignored them because he always treated me like a professional. I knew his wife and their children. It stunned me when he stood in front of the door and masturbated in front of me. That night after I got back to my room, I called a friend in New York to help me get out of my contract with my agent. She gave me Bernie Langston's name. Within a month I was out of my contract and on my own."

"Wow, I don't know what to say. Damn Maggie, do you have any idea how far out of my league you are? Like holy shit!"

"Believe me when I tell you how much you matter to me and how much I'm in love with you. My marriage is a disaster. I want to make sure that bastard doesn't get a penny more of my money."

"Maggie, I'm sorry, I'm at a loss for words."

"As soon as I was on my own, I met my future husband. It was the worst thing I could have done. I didn't realize it, but he only married me for my money. Thank God I met Bernie Langston, who besides getting me out of a contract with my agent, he put together a plan to make sure my money stayed with me. When I first met my husband, he was trying to start his own practice. He wasn't happy being the in-house gastroenterologist for a small hospital north of town. It amazed me how much he already knew about me. Now, when I think about everything he knew, it's so creepy he researched my career and me. I don't understand why I didn't realize it. I bought everything he was selling. Six months after we met, we flew to Las

Vegas and got married. It turned out to be the biggest mistake of my life."

"I'm glad you're getting divorced."

"If you know a mean ass divorce lawyer, let me know," asked Maggie.

"You're asking the wrong person," I answered. "When my ex filed for divorce, the only question anyone asked was what took her so damn long. I didn't hire a lawyer and gave her and my son everything we had. She was right in divorcing me after I messed up our marriage. If you think I did her a favor by giving her everything, understand, we didn't have a damn thing. I took on all the debt. Do you still want my opinion on divorce lawyers?"

"Have you ever heard of a lawyer named Penelope Bergdorf?"

"Can't say that I have," I answered. "Why?"

"A friend I know mentioned her name. I thought you might have heard of her, that's all."

After Maggie fired her manager, she swore that she'd never find herself in that situation again. She admitted that, regardless of all the bullshit her business manager put her through; she became worth over thirty million dollars.

Bernie Langston was the best decision she ever made. He helped her dissolve her relationship with her manager. He then advised her on how to protect her assets from those who would take it all. She took his advice to heart and hired him to help her make her fortune bulletproof from those who had other plans. Later, she would be thankful she had taken the lawyer's advice. It saved her from losing everything to her control-freak husband.

After their marriage, her new husband convinced her to finance his medical practice. After the doctor found out how encompassing the financial arrangement to protect Maggie's money was, he was obsessed with managing her money. The arrangement involved a contract lawyer, an investment manager, a bank and a national auditing firm. The entire agreement aimed at ensuring not only protecting Maggie's funds but also the use of her money to enhance her net worth. Fuming with fury, Maggie's husband stumbled upon the true extent of this arrangement. He learned he would have no say about her finances until their tenth anniversary. Even then, all the principals had to have a unanimous vote to include him in the arrangement. The doctor became incensed when learning that he had to wait ten years to be part of the financial arrangement.

He tried to circumvent the financial arrangement by appealing to Bernie Langston man to man. It didn't work. Even when the doctor showed up at his office unannounced, the lawyer refused to even meet him. It incensed the doctor not to have access to Maggie's money.

Maggie had agreed to finance his medical practice. She realized he insisted on having complete control of the eight million dollars allocated for his new clinic. At her husband's insistence, Maggie scheduled a meeting. Bernie explained that, to spend that amount of money, required an audit of the proposal for the new medical practice. The audit assured the doctor used the money for the project wisely. He explained his firm would follow the instructions of the auditing firm. Bernie would oversee the costs related to setting up a new medical practice. To receive funding, the doctor must develop a business plan and explain all expenditures. Bernie Langston's law firm approved and paid all bills through his office. His office would approve and buy all equipment and pay all invoices.

The doctor threatened to fire Bernie Langston. Bernie explained that the agreement is binding under civil and criminal law. It would take months, if not years, to dissolve. The doctor learned he had no control over the financial agreements.

There was a clause that required both the lawyer and Maggie's approval for funds over two hundred thousand dollars. Bernie could object and delay any transaction deemed unsound.

Maggie didn't realize that he was such a control freak. She also learned that her husband had uncontrollable fits of rage. As they drove home from the lawyer's office, her husband hit the steering wheel so hard, he broke a bone in the palm of his left hand.

She told me about the first time we met in the park. She explained her husband had punched her in the face just before leaving for work. They'd argued that morning about not getting home until after midnight. She felt so humiliated when she discovered her husband was a serial womanizer. He had lied to her from the first day they met. Taking control of her entire fortune was the doctor's only reason for marrying Maggie.

· · · ·

I'm standing on a sidewalk on North Rosemont Avenue. It's after dark, and I see Maggie walking toward me. "What's going on?"

"Hey Jack, you're having another dream," said Maggie. "How's your trial going."

"Why are you in such a hurry?"

"Because I'm late and I hate being late. So, are you going to answer my question or not?"

"I forgot. Did you ask me a question?"

"How did your trial go today?"

"Oh yeah, well, my lawyer had my ex-wife testify."

Maggie stopped. "Why am I thinking this cannot be a good thing?"

"She was sweet. Why are you walking so fast?" I asked.

"Like I said, I'm late and hate being late. Being late is both disrespectful and proves you're a prick if you show up late. And I hate being late. So is the jury going to find you innocent?"

"I hope so, but I'm not holding my breath. Would you mind stopping for a minute? I'm getting winded. Who are you going to see?"

"That's a silly question, my sister Elaina and my brother David. I thought you knew that. Elaina is having a dream, and I don't want to miss it. I love her so much. God, how I wish things would have turned out better for my brother, sister and me."

"Oh, thank you for stopping. I thought I was going to have a heart attack. Is Elaina and David your brother and sister?"

"I told you who they are."

"Well, if you don't mind, could you tell me again? I'm sure this is a dream. I see no reason we need to be walking so fast."

"David is my brother. He is the oldest and I'm the youngest. My sister Elaina is between David and I. Poor David died a long time ago," said Maggie.

"How did your brother David die?"

"He was gay, and he died of AIDS. No one should die for being gay."

"I forgot you told me. Why you're rushing?"

"I'm worried about my sister, Elaina. I have to be there for her dream. I just have to."

"Is your sister, okay?"

"I don't know. When David died Elaina, and I took it so hard. He was thirty-two when he died. Then I died, and I couldn't say goodbye to Elaina. I don't want her to feel alone. I want her to know how much I love her. Do you have any idea what it would be like to lose your siblings?"

"Yeah, I know what it's like. It sucks."

Maggie stopped and looked at me, tears streaming down her cheeks. "I'm so sorry."

"That's okay. Are you meeting them somewhere?"

"Yes, we're meeting at The Fourth Street Diner."

Chapter 20

Joe Hammer

"I have to say, I'm glad you've developed a little humility over the past two years. Not to mention you look healthier. Did you lose some weight? Splurge a little and get a suit that fits."

"Yeah, that would be nice, but on my salary, that'll have to wait. It's a humbling experience to realize the only job I could get was mixing paint at a home improvement center."

"Maybe you'll become a decent guy after all? Anything's possible."

"Yeah, what can I say? How's everything with your bible thumping creep boss?"

"Crawl out of your shell, Joe. I'm thinking you don't like my boss."

"I don't and you shouldn't either. He's a pseudo religious snake"

"What are you saying, Joe?"

"Nothing you don't already know. Let's leave it there."

"The other day in chambers with Judge Taylor, you said there was an inconsistency in the police report. What were you referring to?"

"There are several pages missing. It looked like someone told Nichols and Templeton to stop looking in the doctor's direction."

"It sounds to me like you have too much time on your hands."

"When I first read the police report, it looked like they were under some pressure from Eric Warren."

"You have your opinion, and I have mine."

· · · ·

I sat at my dining table recuperating from a call with Penelope Bergdorf. During our brief phone conversation, I explained I was representing Jack Holt. During my explanation, I got the impression she somehow knew all about the Jack Holt case. When I asked her for a meeting, she accepted without hesitation. After hanging up, I thought about the few times I had dated her when we were in law school. The pseudo-relationship ended when Penelope told me she was not only a lesbian, but she wasn't all that crazy about men. She could have ended there, but she explained it was my horrible personality that convinced her she had no use for a man in her life. As poetic justice, or perhaps by my ex-wife's design, Penelope Bergdorf represented her during our divorce. Timing my divorce couldn't have come at a worse time. Three months after losing my license to practice my wife filed for divorce. To Penelope, it was an honor to take me for everything I had. She told me I was an arrogant asshole and deserved all the shit that was coming my way.

My dislike of Penelope didn't impede the meeting. With any luck, she could have information that would help in Jack Holt's defense.

Penelope agreed to meet with one unexplained caveat. She insisted the meeting take place tomorrow at 5:00PM. She insisted we meet at a sleazy, out of the way biker bar on the Southside of town.

• • • •

There was some irony. I still drive the old beat-up clunker, a Dodge Durango. The parking lot was dirt and full of chopped Harley-Davidson motorcycles. As soon as I opened my car door, I smelled the sharp stench of cigarette smoke, garlic, and stale beer. I had quit smoking five years before and had become righteous about my accomplishment. I had little tolerance of being around cigarette smokers. The stink worsened when I went inside. The darkness of the room blinded me. After a few seconds, I could see Penelope waving her hand. As soon as I saw her, I remembered how much I detested her. I put a smile on my face as I made my way through a cloud of cigarette smoke hanging in the air. She was a drop-dead gorgeous, chain-smoking lesbian divorce lawyer. She had a reputation for being a ruthless bitch in defense of her clients. As I got closer, I noticed David Sinclair, a retired quirky detective who worked only for Penelope. They earned a reputation for pushing the limits of the law.

"Well, well, well, look at you. Joe, how's it going?" asked Penelope as she stood up and gave me a bear hug as if we were long-lost friends.

"I'm doing fine," the hug caught me off guard. "How are you doing?"

"I'm just dandy. I understand you already know David, right? Please, Joe, take a seat."

"How are you doing, David," I asked as I extended my hand. "How long has it been?"

"Nice to see you, Joe. It's been a long time for sure. I gotta tell ya, never in my wildest dreams did I think I'd see you as a defense lawyer."

"That makes two of us," I replied.

"It surprised me when you called me yesterday. After your divorce, I thought you'd never want to see me again," said Penelope. "I hope there are no hard feelings. You're a lawyer, you know I was just doing what my client wanted."

"Oh yeah, Penelope, I understand. I had my reservations," I answered as I sat down in the booth. A young scantily dressed gal put a beer in front of me. "After I thought about my divorce and how you represented my ex, I have to admit I may have had it coming."

"How's it feel being on the defense side of criminal law?" asked Penelope.

"It's only been a few days, and I only have one client who's not impressed with me. Since neither of us has other options, we're trying hard to make it work. What can I say? Thanks for meeting me with such short notice."

"No problem, we've got a lot to talk about. Joe, I'm glad that you're getting back in the game. I hope you're successful. I always thought you were one of the smartest guys around, even though you were a bit of an asshole."

"Thanks Penelope."

"Would you mind if I told David a story about you and me?"

"Well, yeah sure, go ahead," I answered.

Penelope smiled, then turned toward David. "I think it was our last year in law school. I'd known him since the first day. We couldn't find a contract law class. Do you remember that?"

"Oh, yeah."

"I was still a good little Methodist girl from San Ramon, Arizona. I was so excited they accepted me into law school. Moving ahead two years, Joe and I started dating. I was still in denial of my sexual orientation. In case you didn't realize it, Methodist frown on one of their congregation who's a chain-smoking lesbian. We dated for almost three months. In that time Joe taught me how to smoke, to appreciate good Kentucky bourbon, and how to have a super magnificent time."

"I don't remember you being a Methodist. I remember teaching you how to smoke."

"You taught me a bunch of things. I don't know why I remember this, but I took the time to look past your horrible personality. Behind his shitty facade, he's a likeable guy, insightful on a lot of topics. Hell, he convinced me to come out to my parents. They haven't spoken to me since."

"Well, I'll be. Huh, so my personality turned you into a lezzie?"

"That can be your claim to fame, Joe." Penelope smiled and lit a cigarette. "We'd better get down to business."

"To set the record straight, I remember you said my shitty personality drove you over to the other side. You were one of the first people to point out what an asshole I am. Are you still a lesbian?"

"Oh yeah," Penelope took a drag from her cigarette. "You know that being gay is not a disease. I had no more to do about being a lesbian than you did about having the world's shittiest personality."

"Touché."

"I suppose we'd better do something. David, and I did a little homework since I talked to you yesterday. I had to make sure you are handling the Jack Holt case?"

"Yeah, it appears I am. Two weeks ago, I was mixing paint. No one was more surprised than me when Judge Horton gave me this opportunity. I'm working for the public defender's office."

"I'm glad you're back in the game."

"Thanks. How about we talk about the issue at hand?"

"Great idea," answered Penelope as she took another drag of her cigarette. "Why don't you start and tell us about your client?"

I told them what little I knew and not only thought he was innocent, but thought he was a scapegoat. He told me that his girlfriend, Maggie Stewart, hired you to handle her divorce. I suspect her weird-ass doctor husband murdered her. That's all my client, and I talked about.

Penelope tapped an unlit cigarette on the table while listening. She lit it, took a quick glance at David, and began. "I represented Maggie for two reasons. The priority was to protect her assets. I had little to do in that regard because another lawyer out of New York did an amazing job of protecting her money. He made it impossible for some shithead like her doctor husband to steal it from her. In the event of her death, her parents and one surviving sister get every dime of her money valued at twenty-six million and change."

"No kidding?"

"No, I'm not kidding. This Bernie Langston, her bean counter lawyer, did an amazing job of protecting her money. As part of the terms of the divorce, I made her a silent partner in his medical practice. The agreement stipulated her husband to make payments of two thousand dollars a month for the next twenty years. I suspected he just might object to the terms of the divorce, so I brought in my old buddy David and asked him to check out our doctor friend. Everybody has a closet, and everybody hides stuff in their closet, it's the American way. David, why don't you share with our new best friend what you discovered."

"David, before you start," I asked, "when and where were the divorce papers served to her husband?"

"If I remember correctly, my guy served the divorce papers to the doctor while he was leaving the downtown Marriot. He'd been having a nooner with a twenty something nurse. It was the same day that his wife Maggie disappeared. Isn't that a coincidence! Joe, you need to hear what David discovered about the wonderful doctor."

David took another drink of beer, then lit another cigarette. "When I checked out Dr. Stewart, the first thing I discovered was he's like you, Joe. He has a reputation of being an incredible asshole." Penelope, without saying a word, looked at Joe and smiled. "It's poetically funny that he's a gastroenterologist."

I smiled while wondering if all these commentaries on my personality were ever going to stop.

"With the help of a few friends, I checked his police record. It was clean as a whistle. As you well know, everybody has a history, so I did a little more research on this guy. He was born and raised in Champaign, Illinois. Both of his parents were on the faculty at the university there. When he was a senior in high school, the local police suspected he sexually assaulted a high school girl. The person who did the checking for me somehow got a sealed juvenile file on a seventeen-year-old Daniel Stewart. I didn't ask the woman how she got into the sealed juvenile records; it wasn't my concern."

While David explained his discoveries, Penelope studied Joe through a cloud of smoke. David stopped talking and looked around the table. "I need another brew. Anyone else?"

"Sure, I'll take a beer," I answered. "Thanks."

"Me too," said Penelope.

David caught the attention of their server, twirled his finger around the table. "Another round." he said before continuing. "After doing more investigating, I found an article in the local Champaign newspaper about an incident that happened at a high school beer party. It never made it to court because it was his word against hers. The bottom line was the police believed poor Danny Stewart."

"What a surprise," said Penelope.

"Three beers coming up," said the waitress as she placed the glasses in front of each of them. Penelope and David both used the opportunity to light up a cigarette. The waitress was on her way.

"My client told me the doctor was a super control freak. Did you find any evidence of that behavior?"

"I'll get to your question but first let me continue. Johns Hopkins Medical School accepted him. He did his gastroenterology residency at Cedars-Sinai in Manhattan. He developed a reputation for having a short fuse and being a control freak. Two times his bosses reprimanded him for his temper. Women accused him on three separate occasions of unwanted sexual advances. One search led me to another; then out of the blue I hit a grand slam."

Penelope smiled at Joe. "Here's the juicy shit. It's so good."

"About a year before he concluded his residency at Cedar Sinai, he met Gloria Bennett. She was an intensive care nurse at the hospital. Gloria and Danny boy got married, but Danny still enjoyed messing around with other gals. Some guys collect baseball cards he amassed sexual conquest of various women."

"Did you offer to tell this information to the detectives working her homicide investigation?"

"Hold on Joe, we're getting there," said Penelope as she turned toward David. "Go ahead."

"A local hospital here in town hired him after completing his residency. He gained a reputation for being a lady's man, so to speak. His wife Gloria found out that Danny boy got a junior nurse pregnant." David took a drink of his beer. "Gloria got a little upset and didn't take the news so well. Who knew! They went through a real shitty divorce. One night, Doctor Danny boy was so pissed at his soon to be ex-wife he beat the shit out of her."

"Hold on a second, David," interrupted Penelope. "Just for the record, I wasn't his wife's lawyer in case that crossed your mind. All right, David, back to you."

Smiling as I took a drink of beer. Even surprising myself by concluding that I was enjoying Penelope and David's company. The smell of cigarettes still stank. I listened.

"As you'd expect, someone called the police and Doctor Danny boy got himself arrested. An ambulance took Gloria to North Mountain Hospital, where the doctors treated her for a broken jaw and two broken ribs. The reason I brought this up was Doctor Danny, unbeknownst to anyone else, had a friend in the DA's office. Would you like to know who the doctor's best friend is in the DA's office?"

"Don't tell me it's Jackson Maynard?"

"It's not Jackson," answered David. "It's the old bible thumper and all-around clean-cut American boy himself, Eric Warren."

"What? Are you kidding?"

"Hold on, pal. I haven't even started the good stuff. Eric Warren and Doctor Danny had some hobbies in common. They were charter members of the Blue-Sky Social Club. In case you're interested, it is an exclusive swinger club for those people with a need for a little extra privacy, if you get my drift."

"Again, David, I'm sorry to interrupt," said Penelope. "I'm glad I'm not a defense lawyer having to deal with anyone from his office.

Eric Warren is a sneaky bible thumping lying asshole. I wouldn't trust him any further than I could throw the son-of-a-bitch."

"What are you saying Penelope?"

"Did you ever wonder why Judge Horton wanted you to practice again?"

"Yeah, pretty much all the time. I guess I'm losing it, but I don't get what you're saying."

"The Sartori family compromised the District Attorney's office and everything they do," answered Penelope as she turned toward David. "Why don't you enlighten our friend Joe?"

"You are aware of the Sartori crime family?" asked David.

"Oh yeah," I answered, "in name only. I didn't handle organized crime."

"Let me tell you some dirty little secrets. It turns out the Sartori family owns the Blue-Sky Social Club. As you know, this family runs drugs, prostitution, and you name it. Here's an abbreviated backstory about the Blue-Sky Social Club. It's owned by a holding company incorporated in Costa Rica," said David, taking a sip of beer and a drag from his cigarette. "It is a private offshore corporation most likely owned by the Sartori family. These guys in the Sartori crime family play for keeps. I heard they have videos of our DA having his knob polished by a young woman."

"Really?" I responded. "Not knowing how to respond to that. Do you have the video?"

"Not yet, but I'm working on getting a copy. They're using this video to get their way in the DA's office. Rumor has it they also have a video of Doctor Stewart at the same club."

"Holy shit, are they extorting the doctor too?" I asked. "Is that why he wanted control of Maggie's money?"

"Beats me? Our favorite doctor's practice is bigger and better than it's ever been. I have a hunch that something is going on behind the scenes," answered David. "While Penelope was setting up everything for Maggie's divorce, her doctor husband had his own agenda. The doctor was pressuring Bernie Langston to put him in control of Maggie's money. Why would a guy who's making a boatload of money insist on controlling his wife's money? Could it be because he's a control freak or because the Sartori family is extorting him? I'll find out, but I'm not doing it for free."

"I understand, but my client is broke, and I'm not any better off than him. The public defender's office operates on a shoestring. Is there any way we could work some kind of deal?"

"Joe, you lost everything during your divorce because," Penelope stopped to consider her words, "it's fair to say you appear to have liked the young ladies as much as Eric and the doctor."

"Yeah, well, that's changed a lot," I answered. "I'm still kind of an asshole, but I'm getting much better than I used to be. Can we work something out for my client? They charged him for crimes the doctor committed."

Penelope looks at David. "I don't want anyone to know this. Okay? I'll pay for you to get as much as you can on doctor shithead. Are you okay with that, Joe?"

"Oh yeah, thank you, Penelope."

"As it stands your client will take the rap," said David. "That doctor is as guilty as hell. Anyone with any sense at all knows. I think there's some kind of relationship between the Sartori Family, Eric Warren, and Dr. Daniel Stewart. This will be a pro bono investigation unless someday I need some free legal work. Just promise me one thing."

"Sure."

"Try not getting disbarred before I need your services." David grins and lights a cigarette.

"I'll do that, thank you!"

Penelope leaned in toward me as if she was telling me a secret. "Everything David told you is inadmissible because he may have got the info under the table, so to speak. The thing is that this information will no doubt lead to something or someone that will give you information you can use in court. The fact is both Eric and the doctor like to screw around."

"I worked with Eric for a long time. He comes across as a goody two-shoes bible thumper who's always quoting some fricking bible verse. I can't believe this."

"Are you serious? You knew nothing about this jerk?" asked Penelope. "How long did you work with him? Those bible thumpers with their patronizing smiles are the most spine-chilling guys around. And people wonder why I'm a lezzie."

"How do you know this?" I asked.

Penelope glanced at David and smiled. She turned toward Joe. "Are you serious? Eric is creepy and has always been creepy. I don't want to hurt your feelings, but perhaps you were too busy kissing his ass to see how creepy he is."

"Joe," David Sinclair looked around the bar. "One of the last cases I investigated was a hitman for the Sartori Family named Carlo Ricci. My partner and I spent a year tracking every move that guy made. We investigated two mid-level cocaine dealers found murdered in a downtown alley. It looked like a professional hit. Spending most of my career watching and collecting information about the Sartori's and their operatives. We knew for a fact that Carlo Ricci has murdered three people. I know but can't prove he killed these two dealers on the orders from the Sartori family."

"If my memory serves me correctly, Judge Horton mentioned Carlo Ricci during a conversation. He didn't explain why, but he had Mr. Ricci in his cross hairs. I don't understand where you're going with this," I said. "What's your point?"

"The Sartori Family has Eric by his balls. We couldn't touch them as long as Eric was the DA. We arrested Carlo at his home, and before that evening, he was out on bail. By the next morning, Carlo was long gone. We got in touch with Interpol and had them do some checking for us. Security cameras recorded Carlo Ricci at Heathrow Airport, catching a flight to Milan. In checking his flight schedule, Interpol learned Palermo was his eventual destination. Security at Milan-Malpensa International Airport recorded Carlo arriving, but he disappeared. We suspect Carlo ended up sleeping with the fishes at the bottom of the Ligurian Sea. The Sartori's don't like people who leave trails."

"No kidding," I responded.

Penelope had a big smile and began, "I suggest you talk to Judge Horton and tell him what you found out. I doubt he'll ask you where you got the information about the DA. My guess is that Judge Horton is using you to get to Eric Warren. Unfortunately, your client is nothing more than bait to catch a bigger fish."

"I hear you. I don't understand why he's going to court. My client is taking the rap for the doctor," I answered, taking another drink of beer.

"Just tell him your sources have a ninety percent chance of getting a video of Eric Warren getting a blow job. You know better than I how to use extra-legal information and the media."

"Before I go to the judge, I want possession of the video of both Eric and the doctor," I said. "Do you have any idea how long it will take to get a copy of the videos?"

"Most likely two days," answered David. "I'll tell you when I know."

"Thanks to both of you."

. . . .

"Hey Joe, how's it going?" asked Jackie.
"One day at a time. How are you? Are you keeping busy?"

"Keeping busy is never an issue in the public defender's office. How's your case coming along?"

"I'm getting to know my client. I wondered if I'm not over my head."

"Is he difficult?"

"No, not at all. It's more me than him. I'm having a hard time not thinking like a prosecutor. To answer your question, he seems like a decent guy. I'm learning the hard way to be a defense lawyer. I have to confess it's a lot more difficult being a defense lawyer than I suspected."

"Are you doing okay?"

"Yeah, it's a challenge. I told my client right up front a lawyer review panel disbarred me for prosecutorial misconduct. He seemed to be okay with it. Like it or not, we're stuck with each other. He's stuck with me because he has no choice, and I'm stuck with him because it lets me do the only thing I know how to do."

"It has to be difficult for you. Your reputation as a prosecutor who fell from grace and your client's facial disfigurement are putting both of you center stage. Have you thought about that?"

"Oh yeah. Look Jackie, all I can do is work hard and smart to represent my client. I have a hunch that Jackson Maynard is leaking information to the press."

"Do you know that for sure?"

"No, but Jackson was my apprentice when he first started. That's what I did when I was a prosecutor. When I had a weak case, the local press loved the breaking news I leaked. Asking some expendable low-level lawyer wanting to make a name for himself to leak information to the media. I'm not proud of it, but that's what I did."

"That was the most irresponsible thing your office did."

"Yeah, it was just one of the many chickenshit things we did. Jackie, that's all history I'm doing my best to move on. My client, although not perfect, he's my only client and I believe he's innocent.

I can't get bogged down with what the local news guys are saying. There's not a lot I can do about it other than do my job and ignore all the noise."

"What else do you have?"

"My client seems to be a well-informed guy who understands our legal process. The more we talk, the more I'm convinced of his innocence. The more I get into this case, the more I'm convinced both the prosecution and especially the detectives were being lazy or pressured. My client has a significant facial deformity. He swears the moment the detectives saw him he became the prime suspect of their investigation. Jackie, I have to admit I'm not so sure that he's wrong. During our last meeting, he said that he and Mrs. Stewart were having an affair. He mentioned that she'd been working with Penelope Bergdorf, a divorce lawyer."

"No kidding. I don't know her that well, but she has one hell of a reputation as a divorce attorney."

"Trust me, I know firsthand how ruthless she can be. My wife hired her, and I got the screwing of my life."

"Oh my, I didn't know that."

"It turns out my ex-wife had the same opinion of me that most of my colleagues do. My client shared all the details of the relationship between the doctor and his wife. I called Penelope to see if she'd meet with me to discuss the work she did for Maggie Stewart. To my surprise, she not only agreed to meet, but she brought along a former detective, David Sinclair. We met in a biker bar yesterday afternoon. They gave me a lot of information that I doubt they'll let me use in court, but I'll try it again. They also discovered the Sartori Family is blackmailing Eric Warren."

"Are you serious?"

"Yes, I'm serious. It turns out there's a connection between the DA and Doctor Daniel Stewart, Maggie Stewart's husband."

Jackie looked stunned. "He's, my gastroenterologist. That's wild?"

"The more I learn about him, the more I think he killed his wife, not my client."

"Have you given this information to anyone else?"

"No, but I think I understand why Judge Horton wanted me on this case. David Sinclair told me he could get videos of Eric Warren having sex at the Blue-Sky Social Club."

"Hold on, you just gave me a big pill that's hard to swallow. Are you telling me the Sartori family is blackmailing Eric Warren, our district attorney?"

"Yes, there appears to be a ninety percent chance. That's what I'm saying," I answered. "That explains a lot of weird stuff that's been going on for the past few years."

"No kidding. Like you getting disbarred."

"I didn't get disbarred because of prosecutorial misconduct. I got disbarred because I was a stark raving pretentious asshole that got in Eric's way."

"How did you find the video of Eric?"

"My client told me that Maggie Stewart was filing for divorce. Penelope Bergdorf was Maggie's divorce lawyer."

"Holy shit, no kidding? It sure is a small world."

"She was also my wife's lawyer when she filed for divorce."

"Damn Joe, talk about shit for luck."

"Yeah, I could complain, but as you know, all that awful shit that happened to me. I had it coming. So, yesterday at a biker bar with Penelope Bergdorf and David Sinclair, we concluded with David saying he could get me a video of both Eric Warren and maybe Dr. Stewart having sex. They think the Sartori family is blackmailing both men. David suspects that's why Judge Horton readmitted me to the bar. Penelope thinks my client is being used to lure Eric Warren into a trap."

"That's amazing, it's almost too much. Was Dr. Stewart involved in any sexual shenanigans?"

"All he could say for sure was Maggie disappeared the day Penelope had Dr. Stewart served with the divorce papers. This all happened on the same day his wife Maggie disappeared. Penelope's investigator said a few days before the doctor pressured Bernie Langston. He wanted complete control of all of Maggie's money. It didn't work. It turns out that Bernie, Maggie's financial advisor, is like a junkyard dog in protecting Maggie and her fortune."

"Sorry to interrupt, but I need a cup of coffee. Let's go down to the coffee shop on the first floor."

"That sounds like a splendid idea," I answered.

After getting settled in the coffee shop, their conversation resumed.

"I asked Penelope if she reported Maggie missing. She told me she thought Eric Warren was a snake, that she wouldn't trust him any further than she could throw him. Between Penelope Bergdorf and David Sinclair, they filled me in on the relationship. Dr. Daniel Stewart and Eric Warren enjoy the pleasure of much younger women."

"What happens now?"

"David told me he would have a video of Eric Warren with a young woman giving him oral sex in as little as two days. Last night at home, David Sinclair called me to let me know his source will share the video with Judge Horton through an untraceable email account. To make a long story short, I'm meeting with Judge Horton tonight and I intend to tell him about the video. I'll inform him that my source would only send it to his email account. I'm out of the loop. David Sinclair didn't find any concrete evidence against the doctor."

"That's incredible. I've only met Eric Warren twice. I thought he is a super religious kind of guy?"

"Oh yeah, I thought the same thing. I've known him for over twenty years. I know his wife and kids. He presented himself as a very spiritual kind of guy. He was always certain that God was on his side. I worked with him and for him almost my entire career. I would have bet money that he was the real deal, but if there's any truth to what I heard, Eric is in a big dangerous mess."

"Okay, Joe, I appreciate the effort you're putting into this case. At the risk of sounding condescending, I'm so proud of you."

"My client believes because of his facial disfigurement; the jury will convict him. The sad part is, I'm not too sure he's wrong."

"When does the trial start?"

"In five days. I've got a lot of work to do."

"Are there any issues relating to your defense strategy?"

"Everything is coming together fine. When I'm done here, I need to contact Jack's ex-wife to see if it makes any sense for her to testify. I think I'm doing everything possible to help my client."

"Okay, let me know if you need anything."

· · · ·

"Hello," answered Alison Cooper.

"Mrs. Cooper, my name is Joe Hammer. I'm a lawyer who is defending your ex-husband."

"I wondered if you were planning to call me."

Her comment surprised me. "So, you know about your ex-husband's situation?"

"I sure do. Two weeks ago, I received a call from someone in the Marsh County District Attorney's office. They wanted to know if I'd give a deposition for them to use at Jack's trial."

My heart sank as she talked. "Do you mind talking to me?"

"No, not at all. I told the clerk yesterday that I had nothing bad to say about my ex-husband. Our marriage went down the drain, but we split amicably."

"Jack did not want me to get you involved," I said. "He mentioned that the marriage breakup was all his fault."

"That's true, it was his fault. Everything bad that happened between us was his failure. I just couldn't reach him and tell him his face made no difference. I loved him, but I could never convince him he mattered to me and our son."

"You split on friendly terms?"

"We did. Jack brought a lot of baggage to our marriage. He had a hard time believing I loved him because of the damage to his face. We remained married for almost four years. It was difficult on both of us. When we first got married, I didn't realize how much he went through when he went out in public. Not one time did Jack and I go out in public that some creep couldn't stop gawking at him. We seldom went out to dinner to restaurants other than The Fourth Street Diner. We never knew which restaurants would sit us in back out of view or sometimes not wait on us at all."

"I don't understand. Why wouldn't you call the manager of the restaurants?"

"The first rule of eating out at restaurants is to never complain to the manager. Yeah, I know, the manager will make sure you get waited on and he or she will make sure the staff takes excellent care of you. The downside is you're never sure what the staff put in the food when the manager isn't looking. I don't want to misspeak it didn't happen all the time, in fact it rarely happened. It most definitely happened, and when it did, I could see the torment in Jack."

"Did the person who called you from the prosecutor's office tell you about the charges filed against Jack?"

"Yes," Alison answered. "Olivia O'Toole, a mutual friend, told me what they accused Jack of."

"You know that he's facing life in prison for first degree sexual assault and first-degree murder?"

"Yeah, like I said, I heard everything. For the record, I know Jack well and there's no way he would have done those things. There's just is no way that he raped and murdered that woman. I'll be the first to admit he was a royal pain in the ass as a husband, but he was no murderer. In fact, he wouldn't hurt a fly."

"Wasn't he taken into custody for domestic violence?"

"First, he never hit me or anybody else. He was drinking a lot in those days. He couldn't hold a job and didn't have the strength to fight back. The night the police took him in; I had fallen down holding our son and got a big shiner. When Jack came home, he was drunk, and we got into another fight. One of our neighbors called the cops. They knew we'd been arguing, and they noticed my black eye and concluded that Jack gave it to me. I told them I fell, but they thought I was protecting him. He spent the night in jail. The next morning, I went to the police station and convinced them he didn't cause my black eye. That's all that happened."

"Would you be willing to testify to that in court?"

"I would do anything to help Jack," answered Alison. "I've heard that he got his act together and seemed to be happy the year before they arrested him. Olivia threatened his new girl-friend Maggie because she thought the woman was up to no good."

"Hold on a second. Who's Olivia?"

"Olivia O'Toole is a waitress at The Fourth Street Diner, a little cafe. You should talk to her; she's a wonderful person who helped Jack get his act together."

"I'll do that as soon as we hang up. Can I ask you about your son?"

"What do you want to know?"

"Jack was a little vague when we talked about you and your son. Would you tell me about your relationship?"

"Here's another situation where Jack has decided that will cost him in the years to come. Now Jack hasn't reached out to Jake since our divorce. I know for a fact that Jack loves him, and I try to tell my son that, but even so there's no bond between them at all. Jake doesn't hate his father, but he feels nothing for him."

"I don't get it, why?"

"Jack doesn't want to embarrass Jake in front of other kids. Besides, I think in a way Jack feels guilty about the way he acted before our divorce."

· · · ·

After hanging up, I called the cafe to see if Olivia O'Toole worked that evening. I asked the woman who answered if I needed a reservation; the woman laughed.

The Fourth Street Diner was about ten blocks north of Jack's apartment on Prospect Avenue. The restaurant shares the first floor with a hair salon, separated by a staircase that goes up to two apartments. Olivia O'Toole lived in the apartment above The Fourth Street Diner.

I walked in and asked an old woman if I could have Olivia O'Toole as a server. The old woman tilted her head and squinted her eyes as if she was trying to remember who I was. She sat me down at a table and revealed that she was Olivia, then went to the kitchen. A few seconds later, I noticed two women peeking at me through the service window. I could hear the inaudible mumbling of their conversation. Two minutes later, a rather stout woman walked out of the kitchen, wiping her hands with a white cloth towel. She walked to my table and asked if I was the guy who had called earlier asking about Olivia O'Toole. I affirmed it was I who had called and told her that Jack Holt is my client. She smiled and introduced herself as Martha Boswell, then apologized for hanging up on me earlier. "You can see by the joint why we don't take reservations." She said she'd get Olivia.

"I'm sorry for being a little standoffish," said Olivia. "I didn't know who you were. Next time, for God's sake, introduce yourself. Have you seen Jack?"

"Yes, and under the circumstances he's doing well."

"That poor man," said Olivia, "People keep piling it on. I don't understand how he does it. Are you having dinner or are you here to talk about Jack?"

"I'm here for dinner and to talk about Jack if you can spare the time."

"Can I get you a drink?"

"I'll have a cup of coffee, thank you."

"The menu is between the napkin holder and the salt and pepper shaker. Look and I'll take your order when I get back."

"All righty, I'll look. Thank you."

A few minutes later, Olivia returned with a cup of coffee, a glass of ice water, and two sets of utensils wrapped with a paper napkin. "You said you wanted to talk. Here I am."

"Great."

"Can I join you for dinner?"

"Sure, you can."

"Good." She placed the two sets of utensils down on the table. She took my order and, without a word, left for the kitchen. Returning with two plates of food. She looked at me for a few uncomfortable moments. "You look like a Chardonnay kind of guy, am I right?"

"Sounds great."

She returned, "Here ya go. Dig-in before it gets cold. What do you need from me?" asked Olivia as she ate.

"I spoke with Jack's ex-wife. She told me you were a friend of his and that you could offer some insight into what he is like."

"Just for the record, I called both the police department and the district attorney's office. I told them both they were dead wrong about Jack Holt. I told them that Jack wouldn't hurt anyone, much less Maggie."

"Did you know Maggie Stewart?"

"I knew her well. Jack and Maggie came here all the time they were two lovebirds. They enjoyed each other's company. I have to say that it didn't start off that way. When Jack brought her here, the first time I kept my eye on her. I followed her and gave her a warning that if she hurt my friend, I would hunt her down and get revenge. I think I scared the crap out of her."

"How did she take the warning?"

"She didn't say a word, she just had one of those, 'dear-in-the-headlights' looks on her face. I made my point."

"I hear you've known Jack longer than Maggie?"

"There are two studio apartments upstairs. I live in the apartment above the restaurant Jack and Alison lived upstairs above the hairdresser."

"You've known them a long time."

"Oh yeah, I think it was fourteen or fifteen years ago. They were a nice young couple. Poor Jack always had a hard time finding employment because of the damage to his face from the automobile accident when he was a kid. It wasn't a good period in his life. I could see he wanted to do the right thing, but people wouldn't leave the poor guy alone."

"What was Alison like?"

"She was a nice, well-mannered young lady. She became concerned about his coping skills. Sharing my sister Margaret's story about living with Treacher Collins Syndrome."

"What is Treacher Collins Syndrome?" I asked, "Did you say you have a sister with this?"

"Yeah, my sister Margaret was born with Treacher Collins Syndrome. In a nutshell, it's a disorder that affects the cheekbones, jaw, chin, and ears. My sister's face looked like it slanted downward.

She had hearing loss and terrible vision. As bad as her physical problems were, they paled to the cruel way people treated her. I saw my sister teased by other kids and adults. I understood all too well what it was like for Jack after seeing firsthand what happened to Margaret. People were and still are terrible to him. It affected every aspect of his life. Jack was going through the same damn thing my sister went through. People are so cruel."

We talked until the restaurant was filling up with customers. Before I left, Olivia agreed to take a deposition and testify at Jack's trial.

Chapter 21

Oscar Rosenthal – Juror #10

I don't want to let a cold-blooded murderer free any more than I want to lock up some innocent guy because he looks like he'd do the crime. Going into this, I thought our legal system was like what I saw on television. Being a private business owner, I suppose I could have gotten out of being on a jury, but I elected to serve, believing it is my responsibility as a citizen. I don't talk a lot, and the experience of being on a jury hasn't changed that about me. I have to admit, Henry gets on my nerves. He's a bully to the jurors who, for whatever reason, can't or won't fight back. To me, Henry's all bark and no bite, the epitome of toxic masculinity. He and the woman sitting on the other end of the table have caused a lot of unnecessary grief.

"I think we've covered the testimony of everyone who testified for the prosecution," said the foreperson. "Is there anything we missed?" She looked around the table as everyone agreed it was time to move on. "It's time we go over the testimony of those who testified for the defense."

"I agree," responded Oscar. "Let's make a list of people of the testimony we want to take another look at. When we get a printed copy, then we could take turns reading it aloud."

"Alison Cooper, Olivia O'Toole, and Jack Holt should be on that list," said Mike Shepard.

"We should hear the defendant's testimony again," said Marty Chu. "I'm surprised that Holt's lawyer let him testify. Why? As for his ex-wife and the old lady, I don't see the point of hearing their testimony again, but if everyone wants to hear it, I'm cool."

"I think Olivia O'Toole was nice, but I also think she was speaking from her heart and brought little else to the case," said Kayla Rooney. "I get it. She was Jack Holt's friend. That doesn't say much one way or another to me."

"May I say something?" asked Oscar Rosenthal.

"Sure," answered Kayla.

"I understand what you're saying, Kayla, but I don't see it quite that way. Olivia liked the defendant a lot. That says something about Jack Holt's character."

Kayla interjected her thoughts. "I have a cousin who was a waitress in Santa Monica where O.J. used to have breakfast. She thought he was the nicest person she ever waited on. That's just dandy, but everyone in the entire world knew that dude was guilty. Who gives a damn if he's nice and gives good tips?"

"Be still my heart," said Linda, sitting on Kayla's right side. "You're bad-mouthing another black person. I'm stunned."

"What is wrong with you?" answered Kayla, shaking her head in disgust. "Why do you say things like that? Damn, you got issues."

"We should hear Olivia O'Toole's testimony again. I can see why the defense attorney brought her in to testify," said Alex Molina. "To a certain extent it worked. I understand both points of view and I think we should hear her again."

"What about that young gal who testified?" asked Mike Shepard.

"Are you talking about that nurse?" asked Henry.

"Yes, Henry. As soon as the nurse took the stand the two lawyers were in a heated war of words," said Mike. "As soon as she answered the defense attorney's questions the prosecutor started objecting. I found it interesting how the defense lawyer interjected the intent of her testimony he wanted to get across to the jury."

"And the point you're trying to make is what?" asked the foreperson.

"The doctor was a big-time womanizer," I answered. "When combined with information from the divorce lawyer, it says a lot about Doctor Stewart's character."

"I don't think the nurse's testimony helped or hurt the defendant," said Henry Keller.

"I think it would be worth our time to read some testimony of Alison Cooper. Does everyone agree?" said the foreperson.

Everyone looked around the jury room.

"If everyone agrees, let's move on to the coffee shop owner, Reggie Hardaway. Can we all agree that Reggie the coffee shop owner was an impressive character witness, but I'm not sure he added much to help the defense?" said Marty Chu. "Unless someone objects, I suggest we talk about the divorce lawyer. What was that woman's name?"

"Penelope Bergdorf," answered the foreperson. "I will request a copy of the testimony from Alison Cooper, Olivia O'Toole, Penelope Bergdorf, and Jack Holt. Are we missing anybody?"

"I think you got everyone we need to review," answered Alex.

The foreperson gave the names to the bailiff to have their testimony printed. Returning thirty minutes later with the printed testimony and the news that the judge wanted them to continue deliberations until ten that evening. The bailiff said Judge Taylor wanted the jury to start no later than seven AM and finish no earlier than ten PM.

5:07PM Wednesday

"Please let Mike read through the testimony before your questions," said the foreperson.

Mike Shepard reads the testimony of Olivia O'Toole. "Okay everyone, don't get all pissy on me, I'm not the best reader but I'll do my best."

. . . .

"Would you state your name for the court?" asked the defense lawyer. "Could you also please give a little background as it pertains to this case and your relationship with the defendant, Jack Holt?"

"My name is Olivia O'Toole I work as a waitress at The Fourth Street Diner at 303 North Prospect Avenue. I've known Jack Holt for nineteen years. I consider him one of my dearest friends. A long time ago, Jack and his former wife Alison lived in the little studio apartment across the hall from me. We became friends."

"Have you always liked Jack Holt?"

"I've always liked him," answered Olivia.

"Could you explain your statement?"

"He was not the best husband to Alison. Not only did he have difficulty holding a job, but he also often came home drunk. In those days Jack let his critics, and the gawkers get the best of him. Frankly, Jack was a kind of jerk."

"How so?"

"He brought a lot of baggage to their marriage. He didn't believe any woman could love him. What he didn't realize was Alison loved him much more than he deserved. The poor thing she put up with so much of his nonsense."

"Let me understand something. You said Jack Holt was one of your dearest friends, yet he didn't treat his former wife very well. Am I missing something?"

"I'm a friend not only with Jack, but with Alison. I've remained close to both of them after she filed for divorce. It broke my heart to see their marriage fall apart. It was all Jack's doing. He had such a hard time coming to terms with the way people treated him."

"I don't understand. Why are you so tolerant of his abusive relationship with his first wife? Are you aware that a woman filed complaints of unwanted sexual advances?"

"Yes, I'm aware of that! Doubt that's malarkey."

"Did you know the police took him in for domestic violence?"

"That happened after they moved out of their apartment across the hall from where I live. I know Jack and I know he would never do something like that, never!"

"Why are you so forgiving of Jack?" asked the defense lawyer.

"I've seen firsthand how people treated my sister," answered Olivia. "My older sister Margaret had Treacher Collins Syndrome. She was born into this world with the unforgivable fact that she had several disfiguring facial features. All I can tell you for sure is that people treated her terribly..." Olivia stopped to regain her composure.

"Are you okay?"

"Yeah, it's hard to talk about. Poor Margaret, every time she went out in public people had to gawk at her. It never ceased to amaze me how horribly some people treated her. They were cruel. She was my older sister, who I loved more than life itself. It was frustrating because there was nothing, I could do to protect her. She was six years older than me; I still remember her torment. I'm still haunted by how people gawked at her and how they mistreated her."

"Children can be so cruel?"

"Are you serious? That's the biggest lie we tell ourselves. Kids were seldom the issue. The people who mistreated Margaret were always adults. They sure as hell knew better. The funny thing is adults always act surprised when they say this. That's why I don't trust goddamn people."

"Mrs. O'Toole, please watch your language," said the judge.

"Do you think it's better today than it was back when you and your sister were children?" asked the defense lawyer.

"Are you kidding? Hell no! If anything, it's worse," answered Olivia. "I suppose it was Jack's facial features what drew me to him and Alison when they moved in the apartment next to me. I get upset when I think about how people treated Margaret and Jack. It's not right, we're supposed to be better than that. We're not."

"Knowing Jack, do you think he's capable of doing what they accused him of?"

"No. He's on trial only because of his facial features. That's it, nothing more."

"I object," interrupted the lawyer for the prosecution. "The witness is not qualified to make such a statement."

"May I rephrase the question your honor?"

"Yes, go ahead."

"Do you think these proceedings are being fair regarding your friend?"

"No, not at all. The local news has tried and convicted Jack just for the ratings. Every evening, they parade him to and from the detention center. He's in handcuffs and shackles while wearing that orange prison uniform. It's disgraceful."

"You seem to be emotional about this?"

"You're damn right I'm emotional. Jack is like a son to me. He's done a lot of growing up over the past ten years. When he first brought Maggie into the cafe where I work, I was very doubtful of her intentions. Over time, I grew to like her a lot. Maggie and Jack made a great couple."

"Again, based on how well you know Jack Holt, do you think he raped and murdered Maggie Stewart?"

"Your honor, I object," said the prosecution.

"There's no way in hell he…"

"Your honor would you instruct Mrs. O'Toole to stop talking."

"He didn't do the crimes they charged him with. It's all a damn lie!"

"Mrs. O'Toole please," ordered the judge as she turned toward the jury. "Disregard the last two remarks by Mrs. O'Toole."

"I have no more questions."

"You're up," the judge looked at the prosecution.

"I have no questions."

Mike Shepard looked up. "That's all there is."

• • • •

"I think Olivia O'Toole had an interesting perspective about Jack Holt," said Henry Keller. "I almost felt sorry for him. Just hear me out. I'm sure people bullied Jack Holt and Olivia's sister. People get bullied every day. My heart goes out to both of them and anyone else who has experienced bullying. The fact remains that nothing she said even came close to changing my mind about his guilt. There is no question in my mind he stocked her, raped her, murdered her, and buried Maggie Stewart in the park."

"I couldn't disagree more," said Hassan. "Let's talk about the issues when we're finished listening to everyone's testimony."

Hassan volunteered to read the testimony of Jack Holt's ex-wife. As he thumbed through Alison Cooper's testimony, he asked the jurors if it would be okay if he only read the selected parts. No one objected.

• • • •

"Do you remember the night the police took your then husband into custody?" asked the prosecutor.

"Yes," answered Alison Cooper.

"Could you tell the court what happened?"

"Jake, our son, had an accident on his bike and needed to go to the emergency room. Jack wasn't home yet, and I couldn't find him at any of the usual bars where he hung out. I had to take a cab from our apartment to the hospital about four miles away. We were there for over two hours. Later we walked home for lack of another way to get there. On the way home, I tripped on a piece of concrete and banged up my forehead. I was angry by the time my son and I made it back home."

"Did your husband make it home?"

"Yes, he made it home around ten that evening. He was drunk, which was the last thing I wanted to deal with on that evening. It would only get worse. Not only was Jack drunk, but he told me that once again he lost his job."

Hassan continued reading for a few seconds. He looked up at the jury and shared his conclusions. "Jack's wife explained she lost her temper and started yelling at him. She told the court this was the third time he'd lost his job. The police arrived a few minutes later. When she answered the door, the first thing they noticed was the bruise on her forehead. As she explained, Jack was drunk and standing behind her reeking of alcohol. They separated them to get to the root cause of the situation and take control. I will only read when the prosecutor asks questions." Hassan began reading once again.

"Did they take Jack Holt into custody?" asked the prosecutor.

"Yes, they did?"

"Why did they take him into custody?"

"They suspected Jack was the reason I had bruises on my face and a black eye."

"Did he cause the bruises and the black eye?"

"No."

"Isn't it true that you feel a certain amount of pity for your ex-husband? Is that the reason you're characterizing Jack Holt as an easy-going man with good intentions?" asked the prosecutor. "Jack Holt the same man who women have accused of inappropriate sexual advances. Police took him into custody because they suspected domestic violence. The same man who hasn't even bothered seeing his own son in fourteen years. The same guy who has never paid a penny of child support."

"You're not being fair. It's more complicated than it looks on the surface. The reason our marriage fell apart was the pressure on him and our family. He worked harder than any person I've ever known. He wasn't successful, but it wasn't for a lack of trying. No one ever took him seriously. I know for a fact that those women who accused him of sexual misconduct had ulterior motives. If you bothered reading the complaints, you'd understand why a judge dismissed them. Jack walked away with no charges because he did nothing. Those people accusing Jack of not being a dutiful father don't know what they're talking about."

"Mrs. Cooper," said the judge. "Are you okay?"

Turning toward the judge, "I'm sorry your honor. To answer your question, no, I'm not okay. Every time Jack and I went out in public, someone felt compelled to stare at his face, every damn time. Why? What do they expect to happen when they stare at him? Once a woman even took a photograph of his face. Stuff like that seemed to always happen. Your honor, I don't get it. Why do they always stare? I know it weighed on his mind, but he never complained."

"Your honor, I'm finished," said the prosecutor, walking back to his table.

"Your honor, may I redirect?" asked the defense lawyer.

"Go ahead."

"Please finish your thoughts regarding people staring at you and your husband. I'm interested in the lack of a relationship between your former husband and your son."

"They don't have a relationship, but I wish they did. I know Jack loves his son. He also knows how cruel kids and especially adults can be. I think in Jack's mind he wanted his son to have a normal life. I understand where he's coming from. He loves his son so much that he's willing to give him up so Jake doesn't have to experience how cruel people can be."

"Do you agree with him?"

"No. I've tried for years to have him be part of his son's life, but it will not happen. I try to understand the world from his point of view. I know it's difficult, but I also know that his son doesn't understand why he doesn't visit and develop a father and son relationship."

Hassan finished by telling the jury he was more convinced of Jack Holt's innocence than ever. The jury discussed the relevance of Jack Holt's ex-wife. Was she good for his defense, or did she help the prosecution? As with what seemed to be all issues, the jury remained split on the defendant's guilt.

· · · ·

The defense called Penelope Bergdorf to the stand. Maggie Stewart hired her to prepare for a divorce from Dr. Daniel Stewart. Her testimony was so compelling, the jury felt it would be beneficial if someone read the transcript of her testimony. Oscar Rosenthal volunteered.

"Do you swear to tell the truth, nothing but the truth, so help you God?"

"I do."

Penelope took her seat on the witness stand. "Could you please state your name and what you do for a living for the record?" asked the defense lawyer.

"My name is Penelope Bergdorf. I'm an attorney that practices divorce law."

"Have you ever met Maggie Stewart?"

"Yes."

"In what capacity?"

"She hired me to help her with a divorce and protect her personal assets."

"What do you mean?"

"Just that. Maggie Stewart was worth around twenty some odd million bucks. I don't remember the exact amount, but you get the drift."

"Why did Maggie Stewart want a divorce?"

"May I start from the general to the particular? When couples get divorced, it's almost always the husband's fault. It's almost always the same reason the husband thinks with the little brain in his pants. He was messing around on her and he got caught."

"Other things?"

"Yeah, a lot of things. She wanted out of the terrible marriage."

"Could you explain?"

"Sure. Besides being a womanizer, her doctor husband was a super control freak. The list is lengthy but let me give you an idea of what the doctor was like. Insisting she put dishes in the cupboards in a particular order. Wanting the same order for items in the refrigerator. He'd mark or weigh each item to make sure Maggie didn't take any of his private food. Again, the list is extensive. Is that what you want from me?"

"That's fine, I believe you've made your point. Do you have any idea what Maggie Stewart was doing before her death?"

"Yes, she met another man that made her happy."

"Who was this man?"

"Don't know or care. The only thing I wanted to know was information from her that applied to the pending divorce proceeding. Reminding her all the time I was her lawyer, not her confessor, a sister, or her mother. Maggie worried her husband would try to take her money."

"Did you find any evidence that the doctor tried to get control of her money?"

"Oh, yeah."

"And?"

"Not only was the doctor a control freak, but he demands absolute loyalty. When things don't go his way, he has nasty temper tantrums. Maggie told me that within hours after their marriage, the doctor demanded complete control of her money. He was angry when he couldn't get control of her money. When Bernie, her investment lawyer, told the doctor, it would take at least ten years assuming all the parties in the contract agreed. The doctor went off the deep end."

"Your honor, I object. Her statement is hearsay," said the prosecutor.

"Overruled," said the judge, "move on councilor."

"Do you have any experiences with the doctor that makes you question his demeanor?" asked the defense.

"The day I had Maggie's divorce papers served to him."

"Could you explain?"

"The server I hired served the divorce papers at the downtown Marriott Hotel. He found Dr. Stewart leaving the hotel with some cute young woman. About an hour later, the doctor called me and was yelling at me. I was told that paybacks are pure hell. He was so upset that he was incoherent. Claiming to be personal friends with the district attorney Eric Warren. The doctor said he would make sure that I would never practice law in this state again."

"Again, this tantrum happened on the same day you had divorce papers served. Is that right?"

"Do you remember the date that happened?"

"I sure do it was August twenty-seventh."

"How do you know that for sure?"

"It's the date they served her doctor husband the divorce papers. It was also the day that Maggie Stewart disappeared."

"How do you know that for certain?"

"I scheduled a meeting with Maggie late that afternoon, but she didn't show up. She'd rented an apartment just across the park from where she lived with the doctor."

"Did you call the police to file a missing person's report?"

"No."

"Why not?"

"In the law I practice, people change their minds all the time. That's why I insist on a nonrefundable payment up front."

"Did you think there might be foul play?"

"No. I thought nothing. I think I went out with my wife and had dinner."

"Thank you. I have no more questions."

The judge looked at the prosecutor. "You're up, councilor."

The prosecuting attorney walked in front of Penelope. "Good morning, Miss. Bergdorf."

Penelope smirked, saying nothing.

"I'm curious. What do you know about Jack Holt that would make you a key witness for the defense?" asked the prosecutor.

"Nothing."

"Your entire testimony was about Doctor Stewart."

"Is there a question?"

"I noticed you referred to your wife. Are you a lesbian?"

"I object," said Joe Hammer. "What's the point of your testimony about your marital status or sexuality? What does any of that have to do with these proceedings?"

"Overruled," said the judge. "You may continue. Stay on subject."

"She your honor. I'll get to the point. Did you have a romantic relationship with Joe Hammer while you were in law school?"

"Yes. We dated for a short time. We broke up," answered Penelope.

"Your honor, I'm asking you in the name of fairness to strike Miss. Bergdorf's entire testimony from the record. The testimony of this witness is giving isn't relevant to these proceedings."

"I've ruled on this twice, the testimony will stand."

"Your honor."

"Councilor, please sit down. Don't bring this up again."

"I have no more questions."

Oscar Rosenthal looked up. "That's all her testimony."

• • • •

"That divorce lawyer's testimony was useless," said Ira McMillian. "Does anyone have a clue why the judge would allow her to testify?"

"I think the defense wanted us to know that Maggie Stewart was not happy in her marriage," said Oscar Rosenthal. "She wanted a divorce because her husband wanted absolute control over her and her money. It's a good thing she hired Bernie Langston to protect her money, or it would have been long gone."

"Let's discuss only the testimony that's worth discussing," said Henry Keller. "I vote we cut ninety-nine percent of what that dyke lawyer said as pure bull shit. Does anyone else agree with me?"

"I do," said Ira McMillian. "The last three witnesses for the defense were in my mind a waste of time. What was the purpose of calling the messenger who served the divorce papers?"

"The defense subpoenaed the messenger to establish an important time," said Kayla Rooney. "Her lawyer told Mrs. Stewart that a messenger was serving the divorce papers at noon. They knew the doctor always had lunch in his office doing paper/computer work. The kid they hired to serve the papers was resourceful. When he tried to serve the papers to the doctor at his office, he found out that the doctor wasn't available. Like all good servers, he had his ways of learning things. He learned the doctor was five blocks away at the downtown Marriott Hotel having a scheduled nooner with a nurse."

"I still don't understand," said Ira McMillian.

"Gee, what a surprise," responded Kayla. "I think you just don't want to believe anything that will contradict the conclusion you've already drawn."

"Whatever. I especially didn't like the part when Jack Holt said he felt sorry for the victim," said Ira. "I could hardly hold back my laughter at such a ridiculous statement. I missed the point when his lawyer asked him if he could catch a yellow tennis ball with his left hand only," said Ira McMillian. "What was that supposed to prove?"

"Are you kidding? Were you not listening to the testimony?" asked Kayla, "The coroner stated that Maggie Stewart's cause of death was strangulation. The murderer left two distinct marks on her throat. The defendant could not have done that because his left arm and hand have severe atrophy. That means it was impossible for Mr. Holt to have killed Mrs. Stewart in that manner. That makes him innocent. What the hell do you not get?"

"I don't believe the defendant when he said he has whatever the hell atrophy is," Ira responded.

"Sometimes this entire process reminds me of the Twilight Zone. Oh my God, I'm thinking all you want is to convict him regardless of the evidence that proves him innocent," said Kayla. "Why don't we ask the judge if we could not only convict him, but let us take him out to the parking lot and kill him ourselves? I'll bet you, Henry, and Linda would get off if we could do that."

"What the hell did I do?" said Linda.

"Look at you. Another black woman with a shitty attitude and a big mouth," said Ira McMillian. "I'm believing you people don't have the ability for critical thinking."

"I'm going to ignore that racist and stupid remark," answered Kayla as she stood up.

"Okay, that's enough. Not another word from anyone." The foreperson went just outside the jury room to discuss the situation. She insisted the other bailiff go into the jury room to ensure no violence broke out between the jurors.

"She told the bailiff the jury needed to take a break. The jurors were losing it with each other. I think it would be a splendid idea if we broke for the day."

After explaining what was going on with the jury, the judge agreed with a caveat that the bailiff talk to both Henry Keller and Linda Sawyer. The bus took the jury back to the hotel.

Even though they'd been warned several times that night at dinner, Henry and Linda lobbied for a conviction. I hadn't changed my guilty vote, but it didn't mean I wasn't listening to differing opinions. I couldn't stop thinking about Jack Holt and Maggie Stewart. What if the claim that they were lovers was true? Is something like that even possible? Could a woman as beautiful and successful as Maggie Stewart fall in love with a guy like Jack Holt? I keep going back and forth on the defense's claim. Listening to Henry, Linda, or Ira's opinions, there are zero possibility: they are lovers. The other jurors half agree they could be lovers.

I'm a mechanic. I do not feel comfortable making life and death decisions. My wife, Frances, and I met in high school. I remember having the same feelings that Olivia claimed the defendant had about his former wife. People couldn't understand what Frances saw in me, either. It is possible that men don't understand women.

I was a terrible student from kindergarten through high school. I just didn't get half of the stuff they were talking about. When I took an automotive repair class at the vocational part of our high school, I was, for the first time in my entire life, an 'A' student. I couldn't contain my excitement as I discovered my passion, a place where I could excel and receive recognition.

Girls in high school terrified me. I would never in a million years have conjured the nerve to ask Frances out on a date. She kept bumping into me and finding reasons to strike up a conversation. I didn't get it for the longest time until a friend of mine told me that Frances had a crush on me. I knew he was pulling my leg because a classy girl like Frances would never have feelings for me. He swore on a stack of Bibles he heard from a reliable source she liked me. I still found it hard to believe. To this day, after being married to Frances for twenty-three years, I'm believing she has feelings for me. Why is it so difficult for us to believe that Maggie and Jack could be a loving couple?

When my sister gave birth to her first child, our family was both elated and shocked at the same time. My nephew Ray was born with a cleft lip and palate. Everyone in our family was having a tough time coming to terms with my nephew's facial anomaly. Not my sister Alice. It took her less than five seconds to fall in love with her newborn son. She clarified any potential issues. If anyone friend or family has a problem with her son; they were to leave and never come back. Nineteen years later, my nephew Raymond is a talented man who works in my garage. Thanks to a lot of dedicated doctors, nurses, and support staff, the fact he was born with a cleft lip and palate isn't even a footnote in his life.

When I look at Jack Holt, I can't help but wonder how Ray would have turned out if modern medicine could not have repaired him to meet the demands our society puts on people.

Chapter 22

Jack Holt

"Hey Holt, your lawyer is here to see you."
"Me?"
"Yeah, you. Hurry, I don't have all night."
"Why?"
"Beats me? Get out of the rack."

I put my shoes on and went with the guard to the holding area where my Joe Hammer was waiting. "Is everything okay," I asked after entering the holding cell.

"Everything's fine. Your ex-wife caught up with me as I was leaving the courthouse this evening. She asked if I could set up a meeting to visit you this evening. I know you're pissed but let me tell you everything. She's not only waiting in the main lobby; she brought your son Jake to meet you."

"Come on Joe, I can't see them, it's been too long. It's been fourteen years. No, absolutely not. No way."

"I realize it's none of my business, but Alison came all this way and brought your son to meet you. I know it's awkward as hell, but I think you'd be doing a huge favor for your ex and especially your son."

"No way, that was a shitty thing to do. I haven't paid a penny of child support. Not one time did I ever call him to see how he was doing. Yeah, yeah, I understand that I'm his father, but I never did a thing a real father does with his son. Goddamn it, Joe, why did you do this? You had no right bringing them here. What's wrong with you? Guard, I'm ready to go back to my cell."

"Hold on guard." Joe waved the guard off. "First, I didn't do a thing. She stopped me in the parking garage. What was I supposed to do? She didn't have to testify, but she did. Her testimony was pivotal in your defense and just might have saved you. If you're half the man

I think you are, you'll suck it up and meet with them. You know I'm right, and you know you have to see her and your son. Running off and hiding in your cell is what a coward does. Is that what you are, a shitty little two-bit coward?"

"Ah, come on, Joe. Why are you doing this?"

"What's it going to be? They're waiting out in the visitor's lobby. I told them I needed to talk to you about the trial before I could let them visit with you. You should see them, it would help your ex-wife, your son Jake, and you too. Here's the deal: I will get them and bring them here to see you. You'll only have twenty minutes, so you need to make the most of it. I would encourage you not to mess this up."

"Oh man, Joe!"

"Yeah, Jack, whatever. It's your damn fault. I told you what an jerk I am the first time we ever met. Besides, you know I'm right. So come on, man, do the right thing and see your son. I know you want to. What do you say?"

"The reason I didn't see him..."

"Hold on, buddy! You don't owe me an explanation. Okay? The only thing I need from you right now is your permission to go get your ex-wife and your son. What do you say?"

I took a deep breath and gazed down at the floor. "Ah shit, you're right, I'll see them. Just so you know, you're an ass!"

"Gee whiz," Joe responded. "What a revelation. Not one person in my entire life has ever called an arrogant ass. Now you hurt my feelings!"

· · · ·

Being so restless, I thought I might vomit. I began walking back and forth across the holding cell. My stomach hurt and felt terrible. The longer I waited, the more anxious I felt. I started hearing the echo of metal doors creaking open and slamming shut. I listened as the footsteps became louder as they approached the door to the holding cell. There was silence for a few seconds as the guard unlocked the metal door to the holding cell. The door opened. There stood Alison and Jake. After a few anxious seconds, they walked into the holding cell. I couldn't catch my breath. I noticed my son trembling and not looking in my direction. Alison looked as though she was about to crawl out of her skin. I stood up to meet them and tried to smile as they entered.

"Hello Jack," said Alison with a bit of trepidation and a trembling voice. She turned sideways to introduce Jake to me. She cleared her throat. "Jack, this is Jacob, your son."

"Oh, boy, you've grown since I last saw you," I said as I patted my son's back. My eyes welled up. "I'm sorry we're meeting here under these circumstances."

"That's okay," answered Jake. "I'm not sure what I'm supposed to say. I've been trying hard to remember you, but I don't."

"Jack, I'm so happy you're meeting our beautiful son. I wish it were under different circumstances, but I'm so happy we could meet each other."

"Hello Alison?" I said, "thank you for all the nice things you said during your testimony."

"You're welcome, I'm glad I could help. Besides everything I said was the truth."

"Well, it was very kind of you," I said. "How have you been?"

"I'm fine. I hope you don't mind us going to your lawyer to see you for a few minutes?"

"No, no, that's not a problem. It's nice to see you both," I answered.

"Yeah," answered Alison.

I turned to my son. "What do you go by Jacob or Jake?"

"People call me Jake. The only one who calls me Jacob is my mom when she's mad at me."

"I can't believe how handsome you are."

"I think he looks like the photographs of your father."

"Yeah, I agree. I think you're right."

"I don't mean to hurt your feelings, but I didn't want to meet you," said Jake. "Mom insisted I come with her. Why didn't you ever call or write me?"

Jack slid his chair away from the table. He glanced up at Alison. Tears were in her eyes as she watched Jack struggle with his son's question. Alison could see his desperation. She walked over and rubbed his shoulder to comfort her former husband. Jack sat up and looked at Jake. "The truth is I don't have a good reason. I'm sorry for the way things worked out. Whatever else it was, please believe it had nothing to do with you. It was me that caused our marriage breaking up. The least I could do was to give your mother and you a clean break. Neither of you deserved to put up with the mess I was back then. I've made terrible decisions in my life, and I'll have to suffer the consequences. Please believe me, I did not do the crime I'm accused of. I've done a lot of stupid things to you and your mother, but I've never been a violent person. I did not murder Maggie Stewart."

"Jack, I wouldn't have put everything on hold to come here and testify on your behalf if I thought you were guilty. Olivia called me and said the police arrested you for murder. I knew I had to tell the jury about the Jack Holt I once knew. I never hated you, even though you were doing your best at messing up your life." She turned her attention to their son. "Jake your father, no matter what happens with this trial, is a good person. Olivia, who we both knew when you were a baby, kept me up to date on how your dad was doing. She told me long before all this mess started that your dad's demons were gone. She said that a special woman named Maggie had helped him grow up."

"Olivia has been calling you all these years?"

"Yes, she has."

"Dad, we've been staying with Olivia in her apartment. She told me everything about you. She even told me what a jerk you were with mom. I don't know you and to be honest, I don't see you as my father."

"And you shouldn't. I understand, I really do. You don't have to explain anything to me."

"I want to get to know you. Mom refused to change my last name from Holt to Cooper. I understand what Mom and Olivia told me about you. They said you were afraid to be in my life because you didn't want people to tease me because of what happened to your face. They also told me that everyone deserves a second chance. If it's okay with you, I would love to get to know you. I hope they find you not guilty, but whatever the outcome, I still want to get to know you."

Tears were streaming down our faces.

"Jack, can we sit down at the table and talk?" asked Alison.

"Sure, I'm sorry I didn't even think of asking. Please sit down. I'd offer you something to drink, but the amenities here aren't so good," I said as I sat down at the metal table. Jake patted me on the back as he sat next to me.

"Olivia told me she liked the woman you were dating," said Alison. "What was she like? I'm sorry I shouldn't have asked you that."

"No, that's okay. Olivia filled you in on everything. Did she tell you she threatened her on our first date?"

"That's something Olivia would do."

We spent a few minutes on how our lives changed, but we focused on our son Jake. He was a senior in high school, hoping to go to Oregon State University. I kept staring at him and marveling at how he looked like my father. After a few minutes, the guard knocked on the door to tell us we had two minutes to wrap it up.

"It seems like we just got here. I wish it was under different circumstances. Jack, I'm praying for you."

"Me too," 'I answered, then turned toward Jake.' "Can I give you a hug, Jake?"

"Ah yeah, that would be nice."

"I'm sorry I wasn't part of your life growing up. Maybe after we get to know each other, you'll let me play a bigger role in your life."

"Yeah, that would be nice. I look forward to getting to know you too."

The clanging of the guard opening the door caught our attention. "All right folks, it's time to call it a night."

Everyone said tearful goodbyes.

· · · ·

"Hey brother, where have you been?"

"I had met my lawyer," I answered as I sat down on my bunk and took my shoes off.

"Is everything okay?"

"Yeah. I'm just tired. The trial is getting to me. All I want to do is stretch out and go to sleep."

"I understand, brother, that's cool."

"Good night, Leto."

"You too, bro."

I reached for my brown-sugar pills. I split one in half and swallowed it. Within a few seconds, I was sleeping.

· · · ·

"Hello Jack, this is Alison."

"Hi Alison. What's up?"

"I'm not asking for child support. I know you don't have the money. All I'm asking of you is to call your son every once in a while."

"If I had any money, you know I would help you out. I'm looking for a job and living in my car."

"Jack, I know you'd help if you could, that's not my concern. I want you to be part of Jake's life."

I listened; no words could describe the shame I felt.

"Jack, are you there? Hello Jack."

I continued to listen without saying a word.

"Jack, please just call your son once in a while to let him know you care."

"I can't. I've done too much damage already. There's nothing I can do for you or Jake."

"Jack, please don't push your own son away like you've done with everyone else. If you exclude him from your life someday, you'll be sorry. Don't do that."

I listened to her sobbing. After a few minutes, before the phone disconnected. I've had this dream a million times.

· · · ·

"When we were getting to know each other, I admired how you told me right up front you'd been an asshole. I heard that conversation, and I have to admit you were right. Jack, I love you with all my heart but holy shit man. What the hell was wrong with you?"

"Cut me some slack, Maggie. I had a lot of problems."

"No kidding? Like a total lack of basic decency."

"I never denied that I treated her terrible. I'll always regret the bullshit I put Alison and Jake through."

"Well, what can I say Jack, we can all be total assholes once in a while. So now what?"

"What?"

"Are you going to have a relationship with your son?"

"Yeah, in the unlikely chance that I'm acquitted. It will be difficult to have a relationship with him if I'm doing life without parole."

"What do you think?"

"About the trial?"

"No, I'm talking about freeing Tibet. Damn Jack, what the hell did you think I was talking about?"

"Well, what are you talking about?"

"I'm asking about the trial. Sometimes I wonder about you?"

"Yeah, well, that makes two of us. All I can say about the trial is that I'm so damn tired of losing weight, worrying, and always being under scrutiny. Only be with you in my dreams is so depressing. I don't know how much more I can take. Let's face it Maggie, justice always goes to the person who can hire the best lawyer."

"I'm sorry, Jack. I don't know what to say without sounding like I pity you because I don't, not at all. You helped me through my darkest hour. I'll be forever grateful. If you want to wallow around in your own crap, that's your business, but don't expect me to be down there with you. Sorry pal, as much as I love you, you're on your own when it comes to pity parties."

"You're right, all this crap that's going on with my life is just getting me in a real shitty mood."

"I have a dandy idea, let's go to Homestead Park. We'll spread out a blanket and take in all the sunshine. We can watch the birds hopping from tree to tree. Watch the clouds meander through the afternoon sky. We can enjoy the smell and the beauty of the flowers along the trails. Who knows, if no one is around, maybe we could get a little side action. We could if we wanted."

Chapter 23

Joe Hammer

My client has insisted that if he goes to trial, he has no chance of an acquittal. Now, since the trial began, he's insisted that I put him on the stand. Considering everything I learned from Penelope Bergdorf and David Sinclair; I'm considering another motion to exclude. If the judge agrees, I'll once again move to dismiss. When I first read the police report, I thought the charges against my client were suspect and on the verge of wrongful prosecution. I'm positive about my client's innocence, which makes me scared as hell of putting him on the stand. Jackson is a talented lawyer if he cross-examines my client. Jack will be in deep shit.

I made my way through the afternoon rush hour traffic to meet Judge Horton at The Old Union Club. David Sinclair told me his contact had received a composite video of Eric Warren and women engaged in various sexual activities on different visits to the Blue-Sky private sex club. Sinclair told me he hired a guy in London to set up a onetime use phantom email address. It cost five hundred bucks to set up an untraceable email address. Emails went through a series of servers between Istanbul, Singapore, and Barcelona before reaching their destination. Sinclair repeated he didn't want the video in any way traced back to him. The best way for that to happen is to send the video to Judge Horton's email account; otherwise, the investigator pointed out, the video would disappear. Sinclair did not want the Sartori family finding out who leaked the video. The Sartori mob had no qualms about leaving a trail of dead bodies to find out who leaked the video. Sinclair also told me he was pushing his luck finding the video of Eric Warren. He would no longer stick his neck out. Sinclair explained I had forty-eight hours to get Judge Horton's private email address.

I wanted to have some concrete evidence putting into question Dr. Stewart's integrity. The news I received wasn't everything I wanted to hear, but it was better than nothing. Maybe Judge Horton could use the video as leverage to convince Eric Warren to resign. After an hour of stop and go traffic, I arrived at The Old Union Club still not sure how to bring up the DA's extracurricular sex activities with Judge Horton.

• • • •

"Hello Joe," said Judge Horton as I entered the judge's private lounge. "I've been hearing some good things about you."

"Hello Judge Horton, that's nice to know. Thank you for taking the time to see me this evening."

"My pleasure. You said you had an urgent matter that you needed to tell me."

"To be honest with you, Judge Horton, I'm not sure how to begin. A man claims to have a compromising video of Eric Warren at the Blue-Sky Social Club on the west side of town."

The judge squints his eyes as he tries to associate the name of the club. "What was the name of this place?"

"The Blue-Sky Social Club."

"That name sounds familiar; I just can't place it?" said the judge.

"It's a private membership club for people into the swinger lifestyle. A private high-end sex club where wealthy couples with the financial means can join and have sex with other people, a high-class wife swapping club. It has an open nonpaying bar that members pay for as dues. They do it this way to skirt the liquor laws that forbid nudity in an establishment that serves alcohol."

"And you're saying someone has a video of Eric Warren at this place?" asked the judge.

"I have not seen the video. I do not know if it is as damning as they claim."

"Why do I care that Eric Warren is at this sex club place? I assume all the members of this private club are consenting adults. We may not care for their interest, but if it's between consenting adults then again, why would I care?"

"They claim to have compiled videos of the District Attorney having sex with different women."

"Okay, we establish that Eric Warren has a rather odd lifestyle. I don't see any laws or any ethics issues. Am I missing something?"

"According to my source, the Sartori family controls the Blue-Sky Social Club through a Costa Rican corporation. It's a front business for their human trafficking trade, prostitution business, and their drug trade. Besides their core business, they also blackmail the members of the Blue-Sky Social Club."

"Is that a matter of fact, or is it a suspicion?"

"Beats me who owns the place. Was it told it's a Costa Rican Corporation? Did the Sartori family own the Blue-Sky Club. I trust my source, but I don't have the means to check it out to my satisfaction. My source says the Sartori's are using the videos to blackmail Eric Warren. They are influencing the entire DA's office. My sources claim that you're a key figure in this super-secret investigation. They said I should make you aware of this new situation regarding Eric Warren."

"My compliments to your sources. If this is true, it could compromise the entire legal system in Marsh County. And you said you have or haven't seen this video?"

"No. My source wants to send the video to you from an untraceable email account."

"Well, what can I say? Where do we go from here?"

"I need an email address from you. I will give it to my source, and you'll get an email within a few hours."

"Something tells me you'd rather not give me your source's name. Am I correct in that assumption?"

"I would rather not, but if you need to know, I will tell you."

"I understand. This source of yours isn't a criminal?"

Joe smiles. "I don't believe so. I used to work with him when he was a detective for the city."

The judge stood up and stretched. "I need a scotch; would you like one?" He walked to the bar.

"That sounds great, thank you."

The judge grabbed a small napkin, then wrote his email address. "Here you go. Excellent job. Neat or rocks?"

"Rocks."

"Atta boy. If things go as I suspect, do you want your job back in the DA's office?"

"You caught me off guard. That was the last thing I was expecting, but it's easy to answer. Thanks for the offer but being a defense attorney is growing on me. The only thing I want is to get my client acquitted. I never in a million years thought those words would come out of my mouth."

"Good for you, Joe." The judge handed me a Scotch.

"Thank you."

"Are you going to get that man acquitted?"

"I wish I could answer that. In all honesty, I don't have a clue. The system discriminates against those who cannot afford to pay. They locked my client up since his arrest and will be in custody until his trial is over. Something is wrong with our judicial system."

"Did your client rape and kill that woman?"

"No, I don't believe he did. He is in jail because the detectives and the prosecutor have prejudged him. Maybe he's the fall guy for a wealthy doctor who's a friend of Eric Warren and also a member of that same Social Club."

"I've also been doing a little homework on Mr. Holt. I don't pretend to know the case nuances like you do, but to me there is no doubt this man is innocent. It looks to me if he's convicted, he'll be taking the rap for a crime the doctor committed."

"Your honor, Jack Holt, is easy pickings. They're after an easy conviction to bolster Eric's run for office next year. I'm afraid my client will appear as their poster boy for a law-and-order campaign next election. I came across this information about Eric Warren when I was trying to build a defense for Jack Holt. Judge Horton may ask you a question?"

"Yes."

"Why did you give me the opportunity to practice again?"

"Eric set you up. Does the name Carlo Ricci ring a bell?

"Wasn't he a hit man for the Sartori family?"

"You're right. His partner was a man named Miguel Acosta. Did you know they were partners in crime?"

"Is it the same person I put away knowing he was innocent?"

"Yeah, same guy different crime. The good doctor put out a contract on his own wife. He hired Carlo Ricci to kill his wife for one million bucks. When the Sartori Family found out the internal hitman was doing a job on the side and the power that be in their family ordered a hit on Ricci.

"We surmised Eric was dirty, but we had no solid proof. My niece was interning at the DA's office when you lost your license. In fact, Joe, she's the person who reported you. She was right to do so. You met her on your first day on the job at the Public Defender's Office. Her name is Hilda Gaspar."

"Oh yeah, I remember her."

"She's still new on the job. She has a moral sense of right and wrong."

· · · ·

Back to my apartment I felt like the world was closing in on me. Even with the positive comments from Judge Horton. The trial was weighing on my mind. Sitting at my small dining table reviewing everything about my client. I turned in early knowing the verdict would happen at moment. Getting up early to visit my client.

"Good morning, Jack," I said as I entered the holding cell. "Your wish is my command. One grande latte with one sugar."

"Oh wow, thanks Joe."

"Because I don't like surprises. Today I want you to tell me everything unfiltered. Tell me everything you know. Let's start with your first encounter with the detectives. Bear with me, remember I brought you the latte so you wouldn't get pissy with me for asking the same questions over and over."

"Well, Joe, since you brought me the latte, I'll cooperate. The best place to start is to tell you when I heard on TV a girl-scout troop found the unidentified remains of a woman buried in the Municipal Park. It was Maggie. Her psycho husband had killed her. The news broke my heart. I knew without a doubt that Maggie was dead, even though they didn't release her name until the next day. I couldn't get her death off my mind. It was the most horrible time in my life."

"Don't you walk through that park every day when you go to work?"

"Yeah, most of the time. When I heard those kids found her body on Saturday morning, I stayed out of the park all weekend. The following Monday, I walked to work by taking the sidewalk on the Eastern edge of the park. I came home that same way. Tuesday, I conjured the courage to walk to work using the main trail the usual way. On the way home I could see the area where the yellow crime tape was still in place from the investigation. There were two guys walking around the scene. I noticed one of them paid a lot of attention to me as I walked on the main trail. Out of nowhere, I heard a screaming sound. I turned toward the direction of the noise just in time to notice one of the two men took my photograph. That shook me to my core. I was so shaken that I stopped and sat on a park bench to regain my composure. That's when I knew they were looking in my direction."

"Really? What made you think of it?"

"Just my intuition, thirty-plus years of experience, and my cynical nature. I went to my apartment, closed the drapes and sat in my living room. It was around six, maybe a little after, when two men knocked on my apartment door. Looking through the peephole. They waited for about an hour before leaving. Then, it dawned on me that my time was running out.

"How did you know it was the police?"

"Someone wandering around a crime scene took my photograph. I had a hunch it was the police," answered Jack. "At the time I couldn't say for sure, but these two guys looked like the guys I just saw in the park. I knew if I answered the door, they would see my face and I'd become the prime suspect. I stood by the door, waiting for them to leave."

"Why did you think your facial features would be an issue with the detectives?"

"Because my facial features are always the main issue to everything that happens in my life. Not to mention my experiences with the police have been sketchy. The bottom line is I don't trust them, and I avoid them. Especially not trusting them when my girlfriend has been missing for a week. I figured they must have found out about our relationship. Maybe Reggie or Olivia said something? Who knows? I knew down to the marrow of my bones the instant they saw my face. Their investigation was over. I have a poor relationship with the police, a lot of which I brought on myself, but not all. I guess the bottom line is I don't trust them."

"Did it occur to you that by refusing to talk to the police without council might have heightened their interest in you?"

"Did it occur to you I might know what I'm talking about when I say as soon as they saw my face, they would have a heightened interest in me? After those two detectives saw me that morning, I was guilty in their minds. I also realize the odds of me getting off is zero. To be honest, I'm not getting out of this mess. Although I doubt, you'll ever admit to it, you know that."

"I don't know that" I answered, realizing full well my client was more right than wrong. "You suspected Maggie was missing and yet you didn't call the authorities. Why?"

"Are you kidding? What did I just tell you?"

"Okay. When did the detectives come back to your house?" I asked.

"You told me you read the police report. Right?"

"Yeah, I read it, but I want to hear it from you."

"On Thursday morning, I was ten steps from the front door of my apartment when they approached me. It was Detectives Nichols and Templeton wanting to talk to me. They asked if they could talk in my apartment. They are asking these questions while we're standing in front of my neighbor's apartment. I told them I had nothing to say without a lawyer and no, they could not enter my apartment without a warrant. At that point they didn't arrest me, but they took me into custody. During the ride to the police station, they tried to get me to talk. I kept repeating that I wanted a lawyer before I'd talk."

"Did they leave you alone after you told them you wouldn't talk without legal counsel?"

"Not really. The conversation revolved around my self-inflicted harm because of lack of cooperation. They made sure I was overhearing their supposed private conversation. They insisted they wanted to talk to me because a neighbor woman had seen me at the home of Daniel and Maggie Stewart on the day Maggie Stewart vanished. My heart sank when they told me a neighbor had seen me. I wanted to tell them I was innocent and had nothing to do with her murder, but I knew better. I've learned not to trust the police under any circumstances. When we got to the police station, they put me in a holding cell. I was there about two hours before a guard took me to a room and gave me my cell phone to call a lawyer. He gave me a phone book and told me I had twenty minutes to call any lawyer. I looked up the number of the Marsh County Public Defender's office. When I called, I got an answering machine. I left a message to them of who I was and that I was being held in a city holding cell. I opened the door to the little room and told the guard I was ready to go back."

"How long did it take to get a call back from the public defender's office?" asked Joe.

"The next morning, some guy called back to get more information about me. I didn't hear until another day had passed. It was around six that evening. They postponed the arraignment so I could talk to my lawyer I'd never met. During the arraignment all the public defender did was stand there while the judge turned down bail. They charged me with first-degree sexual assault and first-degree murder."

"How long did you know Maggie Stewart?"

"Two years."

"How well did you know her?"

"Intimately."

"How did you meet her?"

"I was walking to work and met her along the way. She looked disheveled. When I got closer, I could see she had a black eye. She claimed she fell while jogging in the park. When you have a face like mine you never approach a woman. So, kept my distance to make sure I didn't make her feel uncomfortable, but I could tell she was hurting. I told her to wait a few minutes while I went to Reggie's Coffee Shop and got her two bottles of water and a hand full of bar towels."

"Did you believe her when she said she fell running?"

"When we first met, I didn't know what happened to her. She told me a year later when we became involved. Her hands seemed fine. It was her face that was all banged up, not her hands. I'm not an expert, but it looked to me like someone beat the crap out of her. Whenever I've fallen down, I hold my hands out to break the fall. It didn't look like she held her hands out to break the fall."

"Did she tell you how she got injured?"

"About a year after we met. She told me her husband punched her in the face and in the gut. She said he was angry about not having control over her money."

"Okay, I see. You said you kept your distance because you didn't want to make her feel uncomfortable?"

"My facial features make many people feel uncomfortable. Some women have accused me of unwanted sexual advances."

"Did you?"

"No, not one time have I made inappropriate advances. When I went through puberty, it seemed like overnight I went from being a cute little boy injured in a terrible automobile accident to a slobbering pervert. Believe me, I know better."

I listened, but I couldn't relate to what Jack was saying. I couldn't explain why I felt uncomfortable around my client. "How did your relationship with Mrs. Stewart go from being a casual acquaintance to romantic?"

"We met again a few weeks later while I was on my way to work. I didn't recognize her, but she recognized me. She told me her name and thanked me for stopping to offer help. We talked for a few minutes, and I went to work."

"Did you meet her other times?"

"Over time, we become close."

"Why would police single you out on her murder?"

"I suppose because I'm the modern-day Quasimodo character who is the quintessential creepy looking guy who obsesses over a pretty girl. Just like I've been trying to tell you since the first day we met."

"Did you ever go to her house?"

"Twice. In fact, I was there the day she disappeared. The first time was about a year and a half ago she asked me if I would help her move some stuff around in her house. That's all there was to it."

"Jack, it's your right to ask for legal representation. Realize there are consequences when you refuse to talk and ask for an attorney. Even though it's your right and even though the police won't admit it, keeping silent could cost you. By not talking to the detectives so early in the game, you made yourself much more than a person of interest."

"Listen to what I keep telling you. The instant those two detectives saw me; I was guilty their investigation was over."

"Come on, Jack, stop saying that. Do you believe that?"

"Do you not believe me? You're thinking it's all my vivid imagination."

Looking at Jack, I'm not sure what to think.

"I've lived with this damn face all of my adult life. It's like carrying a bucket load of fresh crap around with you everywhere you go. A bucket that I can't get rid of, it's always an issue whether it's spoken or unspoken. It's right there, and there's not a damn thing I can do about it. Do you have any idea how old that gets?"

I took a deep breath. "I need a cup of coffee, how about you?"

"We can do that?"

"Yeah, I think so. I'll find out."

Ten minutes later I return with two paper cups filled with hot, bad-tasting coffee. "I bought these from one of those machines in the lobby. You know the kind where a paper cup falls in place and this black goop, they call coffee pours into the cup. So, there ya go, Jack, enjoy!"

"A cup of black stuff that smells like genuine black stuff."

"Let's continue. When did you discover Maggie was missing?"

"The day when she didn't return to my apartment. There was no doubt her husband had done something."

Working with all kinds of people over the years, it was hard believing Jack's opinion of the police. I understood it wasn't easy having a facial difference, but my client is blaming everything on the way he looks. It was a predicament, teetering back and forth about my client.

"Believe what you want. If you don't like my answers, don't bother asking the questions."

"Did you have anything to do with the death of Maggie Stewart? What's the actual reason you didn't want to talk to the detectives?"

"If you don't believe me, then go away. I didn't ask for your help. Go hang out with the police officers you seem to admire so much."

"Hold on, I misspoke. I just have a tough time believing some things you're telling me. Here's a news flash... so will the jury! I am doing everything I can to get you an acquittal. We're on the same side. It is hard trying to understand where you're coming from. I have to convince a jury the prosecution's case leaves a reasonable doubt. Please believe me when I tell you I'm on your side."

"Walk in my shoes for a while. You'll find out real fast how much you don't know. The same officers that pull over and kill black and brown people are now pure as the driven snow, with guys who look like me. Who's being naïve?"

Chapter 24

Oscar Rosenthal – Juror #10

I feel old when the foreperson keeps referring to me as Mr. Rosenthal instead of Oscar. When I started law school, I wanted to be a criminal defense lawyer until my second year, when I discovered intellectual property law at lunch with a cousin. She claimed I could make a lot of money without all the stress of a criminal defense lawyer. I worked at her law firm for forty-four years. Until this trial came along, I always wondered if I had made the right choice. Finally, at the ripe old age of seventy-three, I know I made the right choice. I watched the defense lawyer do everything he could to disprove the prosecution's case against Jack Holt. It surprised me the case even went to trial. Since the deliberations began, I've barely slept worrying about the man on trial. I don't see how our jury will ever agree as to his guilt or innocence.

Getting off early the day before didn't diminish the frustration I hoped it would. The stress on the jurors was palpable. The shuttle ride from the nearby hotel was quiet. No one, including myself, spoke or looked at each other as we filed into the jury room. The foreperson asked for a volunteer to read Jack Holt's testimony. Kayla volunteered. She looked as if she hadn't slept the entire night.

Removing her glasses from her purse and inspected Jack Holt's testimony. "Do I need to read everything? I mean, do we need to hear him being sworn in?" asked Kayla.

"That's an excellent point," answered the foreperson. "Just skip the areas you think are unnecessary. If any of us get lost, we'll stop you to clarify."

"Okay, that's cool." She read Jack Holt's testimony.

• • • •

215

"The injuries to your face resulted from an automobile accident, is that right?" asked the defense lawyer.

"Yes, when I was eight years old."

"Would you mind telling us about the accident?"

"The accident killed my father and two sisters. My mother's injury was severe. The collision pushed her legs up into her abdomen, causing irreparable damage to her lower GI track. The impact also severed the spinal cord. She was paraplegic for the rest of her life. I was sitting behind my mother. I survived with the least amount of damage. The force was so strong it broke bones in my left arm, hand, and shoulder, including my left cheekbone. There were three breaks on the left side of my jaw. Besides all my broken bones, the accident damaged my seventh cranial nerve. This caused paralysis on the left side of my face and atrophy in the back of my neck, my left shoulder, arm, and hand."

"Could you explain to the jury how atrophy affected you?"

"Atrophy is the wasting away of my muscle tissue in my neck, left arm, shoulder, and hand. In those areas I have limited mobility and little strength."

"Thank you," said the defense lawyer. "Would you mind explaining so we can understand what's going on?"

"Well, for example, I can move my left arm and hand, but I have little muscle strength and lack of coordination."

"If I toss you a tennis ball, could you catch it with your left hand?"

"No."

"Would you mind trying?"

"Sure."

The lawyer tossed the ball to Jack as he failed to catch it.

Kayla read through the transcript until she reached the next topic.

"The autopsy report stated that a man with two powerful hands choked Maggie Stewart to death. We've all seen the photographs of the wounds on Mrs. Stewart's neck. For clarity's sake, let me repeat. The autopsy report stated that the coroner could identify the bruising that the murderer's thumbs did to both sides of her neck. Mr. Holt, did you strangle Maggie Stewart to death with both of your hands?"

"No."

"Why should we believe you?"

"It would be impossible for me to have murdered her like that. I don't have the strength in my left hand or arm to do such a thing. The fact is, I was in love with her, and she was in love with me."

Snickering from the audience caused a quick response and an angry reprimand from the judge.

"Could you tell the jury about how your relationship with Mrs. Stewart evolved?"

"I've known her for almost two years. It started out as two people just talking about things. I knew up front she was out of my league, so I took our conversations with a grain of salt."

"What do you mean by that?"

"Sometimes there are bleeding hearts that go a little overboard with their feelings. I'm always guarded in that regard. She was nice enough, but I'd rather be safe than sorry."

"Could you please clarify that statement for the jury?"

"Even though most people deny having issues with people who look like me. Most people find my facial features disturbing and want little to do with me. Other people go overboard trying to be nice. At first, that's the way I thought about Maggie. Another bleeding heart. They try too hard to be kind. It's almost like I'm some special do gooders project."

"How did you meet her?"

"I walked to work every day by taking the main trail through Homestead Park. One morning, I noticed a woman trying to stand up from a park bench near the creek. Even from fifty yards away, she appeared hurt. I walked over to see if she was okay."

"Was she okay?"

"No, she wasn't. When I asked what happened, she claimed she fell while jogging in the park. Doubting what she said, I let it slide not to pry. She had bruises on her face but no bruises or damage to her either of her hands."

"What do you mean?"

"To me it seems logical that if someone falls while jogging, the first thing you do to break the fall is hold out their hand. Her hands looked fine to me. I thought someone attacked her. She kept insisting she was fine."

"Then what?"

"I ran to Reggie's coffee shop and got her a couple bottles of water and a handful of bar towels so she could clean herself up."

"Did you call a park ranger or the police?"

"No. I wish I had. She said she lived close by. To be honest, she seemed on top of things. I just went to work. I didn't want her to get the idea I was taking advantage of her situation."

"How did you go from a chance meeting in the park to an intimate relationship?" asked Joe Hammer.

"After our initial meeting in the park, I went on with my life and forgot about her. Two weeks later, I was having a cup of coffee and reading the paper at Reggie's. Out of the blue, this woman asked if I would join her for coffee. She looked kind of familiar, but I couldn't place her. That's bad because she's a great-looking woman. I couldn't help but wonder why she's wanted me to sit with her?"

"Did you ever figure out who she was that morning?"

"Yeah, but only because she wanted to thank me for stopping in the park to offer her help. Then I knew she was the woman in the park."

"Did you meet regularly after that?"

"No, I thought it was nice that she thanked me. After the short meeting, we both went on our own way. Our relationship developed little by little over the next two years."

"When was the last time you saw her?"

"The morning of the day she disappeared."

"Could you tell the jury what happened that morning?"

"I had the day off because Maggie wanted help to move her personal stuff out of her house. She called and said she was nervous and wanted to come over to spend the morning with me in my apartment."

"Why was she nervous?"

"Penelope Bergdorf, her divorce lawyer, scheduled to have the divorce papers served at noon. It was a time when her husband was inside his office. She was afraid of what he would do to her after he received the divorce papers. She came over around seven thirty. We drank coffee, we talked, and then we had sex. At nine straight up, we drove the truck I rented to her house to retrieve some of her belongings. We were there for about thirty minutes before we drove to her apartment."

"If you two were so in love, why didn't Mrs. Stewart move in with you?" asked the defense.

"Her lawyer insisted she have her own apartment while the divorce was going on."

"What else happened that morning?"

"We put things away in Maggie's apartment and went back to my place to get her car. I needed to take the rental truck back. After we finished, we went back to my apartment at eleven-fifteen that morning. We had a little lunch, and once again made love. We were talking when she remembered that she's forgotten her grandmother's jewelry box. She panicked and told me she wanted to go back to get it before her husband received the divorce papers. I offered to go with her, but she insisted it wasn't necessary, she'd go get them and be back in a few minutes. It was the last time I saw her."

"Let's switch topics and talk about the events that happened after Mrs. Stewart vanished. Were you concerned when she didn't return?"

"Yes."

"Did you go to the police?"

"No, but I should have."

"Why didn't you?"

"I suspected that Doctor Stewart had done something to Maggie, but I thought about confronting the doctor in his office. I even considered calling the police, but I couldn't do that either."

"Why?"

"Women have accused me of unwanted sexual advances in the past."

"Did you make unwanted sexual advances?"

"No."

"Can you tell the court what these charges were about?"

"There were four in total. The first time was in high school, a girl went to the principal and said I'd was acting creepy toward her. That was the hardest. I was going through puberty, and I'm a slobbering sex pervert. It was a tough period in my life that took years to get over."

"What did you do to the girl to provoke her to tell the high school principal?"

"When I met with the principal, I got the impression he didn't believe me when I denied everything the girl said I did. He ordered me to stay away from the girl or else. That incident in high school changed me to my core."

"What about the other three women?"

"More of the same thing, not once have I acted that way around women. All the complaints were bogus."

"I have one more question. Did you rape and murder Maggie Stewart?"

"No, I did not."

"No more questions your honor."

The judge looked at the prosecutor. "Your turn."

"Thank you, your honor," said the prosecutor. "I'm curious, I want to make sure I have a correct understanding. Mrs. Stewart was a wealthy professional model, worth millions and known around the world. Are you asking the jury to believe that Maggie Stewart pursued a romantic relationship with you?"

"I'm not asking the court to believe anything. I'm just telling the truth."

"How about I give another scenario," said the prosecutor. "The evidence is obvious that you stocked Mrs. Stewart and when the time was right, you raped and murdered her in cold blood. Isn't that what happened?"

"No. I had nothing to do with Maggie's death."

"If that's true," said the prosecutor. "Why did you refuse to cooperate with the detectives when they came to your apartment?"

"I don't trust police officers. I have the right to remain silent and a right to have legal counsel."

"Mr. Holt, you like to exaggerate things and tell tall tales, don't you?"

"No more than anyone else."

"Could you tell us about your time in the military?"

Jack looked down at his lap, not saying a word. "I was never in the military."

"Really? That's interesting, I have sworn affidavits you told people the injuries to your face were combat related. You'd received these wounds while serving in Iraq."

"Can I explain?"

"Mr. Holt, just answer the question, yes or no. Would you like me to repeat the question?"

"Yes, I did, but if I can explain."

"The question was a yes or no question. You answered, yes. You, in fact, lied to these and other people about your military service. Isn't that correct?"

"Your honor I object to the prosecutions badgering my client," said the defense lawyer. "He's already answered the question."

"Overruled," answered the judge. "Continue."

"Is that correct, Mr. Holt?" asked the prosecutor.

"Yes."

"So, you lied about being in the military. Are you lying now when you deny raping and murdering Mrs. Stewart."

"No. I did not hurt Maggie Stewart. We were in love."

"Your honor, I have no more questions for this witness."

"Your honor," said the defense lawyer. "May I redirect?"

"Go ahead."

"Mr. Holt, why have you told some people you served in the military?"

"I've lived every day with my facial disfigurement," Jack stopped to collect his emotions. His eyes were welling up with tears.

"Mr. Holt, are you okay?"

"I'm fine."

"Could you hold your head up and speak to the court louder so everyone can hear you?"

"Yes. Since the accident, I've never been in public where someone doesn't gawk at my face. When I told people, I'd been in the military, I was trying to reframe the reason my face looks the way it does."

"Why on Earth would you do something like that?"

"If I tell them my face looks the way it does because of military service, it's more socially acceptable. I know it's wrong, but it helps make people a little less judgmental about my facial features."

"Thank you, Mr. Holt. Your honor, I have no more questions and the defense rest."

. . . .

We spent the next hour debating the closing statements of the prosecution and the defense. The tension was mounting as we continued to debate the merits of the trial. Henry and Linda were not cooperating with the rest of the jurors. It remained a struggle between the foreperson, Henry, and Linda.

Their behavior was wearing thin. I couldn't take it any longer. I got up and walked out of the jury room to speak to Gus, the bailiff, who seemed in charge. If that didn't work, I would take my concerns to the judge. Something had to change.

"We have an explosive situation with the jury. Henry Keller and Linda Sawyer have from beginning of the deliberations have undermined the foreperson and the entire jury. The foreperson is taking the brunt of their actions. It is becoming an explosive situation."

Gus listened to my concerns. After I finished, he asked Dennis, the other bailiff, to go into the jury room to make sure everyone is in control of their emotions.

"Mr. Rosenthal. Why don't you come with me to see the judge?" asked Gus. Within a few minutes, we were sitting in her chambers.

"Your honor we seem to have a problem with the jury. Two members, Henry Keller and Linda Sawyer, are bullying the foreperson and the other members of the jury. They are getting pushback from a few, but most have checked out. Mr. Rosenthal thinks it could break out in violence."

"Mr. Rosenthal, what are your concerns?" asked the judge.

"Your Honor, these two individuals are verbally attacking some other jurors for having different opinions. It's frustrating, and the tension is mounting."

Speaking to the bailiff, "Gus, these names sound familiar to me. Why is that?"

"Your Honor, I told you about some racial and ethnic statements Henry Keller made almost as soon as deliberations began. Later the foreperson gave us Linda Sawyer's smart phone."

"If my understanding is correct, these two are being a royal pain in the ass, is that right? And you'd like me to go to the jury room and have a come to Jesus meeting with everyone. Am I understanding the situation correctly?"

"Yes, that's what the jury needs," said Gus. "Your Honor, may I ask why you insisted Janet Fischer to be the foreperson? These two people have directed their nastiness toward the foreperson."

"Gus, you remember when my youngest daughter Melissa was sixteen and in the last stages of bone cancer?"

"Yes," answered Gus.

"Janet Fischer was her nurse. I didn't talk to her much when she was caring for Melissa. I haven't seen or heard from her in fifteen years. This woman left an indelible mark on me, even after all these years. I've never met a more compassionate person. She helped our entire family endure the terrible death of my sixteen-year-old daughter," the judge answered. "Mr. Rosenthal, thank you for bringing this to my attention. Gus will take Mr. Rosenthal back to the jury room. I'll be down to talk to everyone. Before you go, do you know where Dennis put that woman's cell phone?"

"In the filing cabinet in the storage room," Gus answered. "Do you want me to get it for you?"

"No, thanks, I'll get it. I'll be just behind you," answered the judge.

"Thank you," I answered. Gus and I were back in the jury room within a few minutes.

"Excuse me for interrupting," said Gus as we entered the jury room. "Judge Taylor is on her way here to talk to everyone."

"What's this all about?" asked Henry.

"I'll let the judge explain that" answered Gus.

"I don't get it. What's going on?" asked the foreperson.

After a few uncomfortable minutes, the judge arrived. "Good morning. I'll get to my point. I understand that two of our jurors don't play well with others. They used racial and ethnic terms to bully fellow jurors. As you well know, I don't like hung jurors. As much as I'd like to force you to come to a unanimous verdict, our system doesn't work that way. You've been discussing this case for three days. I realize that being on a jury is difficult. When you're discussing a crime of this magnitude and you're seeking justice, tensions often erupt. This is nothing new, in fact we see it all the time. Start over with open minds, try your best to come to a verdict. This is serious business. You have more time to conclude your jobs. Does anyone have questions?"

No one answered.

"I've received complaints about Henry Keller and Linda Sawyer. For your information, Mr. Keller, making racial, religious, and ethnic slurs when talking to other jurors is a felony. Let me assure you it is not only unacceptable if there is another use of insulting racial, ethnic, or religious in these deliberations, there will be severe consequences. Please know I will apply the strongest punishment if I hear one even the slightest complaint. I hope I made myself clear on this matter."

"Who told you this?" asked Henry Keller.

The judge looked at him without a response. "Mr. Keller, do you know how close I am to charging you with contempt of court. This is a serious crime. When the jury resumes, I want you to take your responsibilities seriously. If I hear of you or anyone else making any kind of slur toward another juror, I assure you there will be severe penalties."

The judge turned her attention toward Linda Sawyer. "Ms. Sawyer when I gave instructions to the jury, I included instructions about no cell phone, tablets, or computers in the jury room. The fact is, I gave those instructions twice and both Dennis and Gus gave the instructions." The judge reached into her pocket and pulled out a freezer bag with a cell phone. "Ms. Sawyer: I'm told this is yours. You defied my order about no electronic devices during deliberations. You are in contempt of court I'm fining you five hundred dollars for disobeying my instructions. After the jury comes to a verdict and the jurors are free to go, I want you to report to Gus. I also want you to stop being disrespectful of your fellow jurors."

"May I say something?" asked Linda Sawyer.

"No, you cannot. This is where I talk and you damn well better be listening," responded the judge. "I realize you are passionate about your opinions. And yes, they are opinions, just like the opinions of the other jurors. All of you go back to work and act like civil, respectful adults. It would be a terrible tragedy if you continue to behave the way you have. Go back and do the job the court has entrusted you to do. Are we all on the same page?" She waited for any comments or concerns as everyone remained quiet. "Thank you. Now get back to work." The judge patted the foreperson on her shoulder as she left the jury room.

Jack Holt

"**H**ey Leto, get your ass out of the sack. You know what to do. Put your nose against the back wall and don't move."

"I hear ya, boss."

I walked in when the guard opened the door. Still handcuffed, I waited until he closed the cell door and removed the cuffs. "Sweet dreams," said the guard.

"Looks like you had another long day?" said Leto.

"The lawyers made their closing remarks to the jury," I answered. "Then the judge gave her last instructions to the jury. There's nothing to do now but wait."

"This is the worst part, waiting for those pendejos on the jury to decide whether you go free or to jail. My lawyer wants to settle out of court. He told me if I plead guilty to a lesser charge, they would let me out in five years and if I behave myself two-and-a-half years. I told him I'd think about it. What do you think?"

"My lawyer told me the prosecutor made a similar offer for me to consider. My options were to plea to manslaughter and get fifteen to twenty-five years. The alternative is to take my chances with the jury, and if I'm found guilty, I'll spend the rest of my life in prison. My lawyer thinks the jury will acquit me."

"Oh, yeah."

"Yeah, that's what he says. He doesn't want me to worry. I'm not optimistic. Maybe he's right, but I doubt that will happen. Taking a trip isn't on my calendar anytime soon," as I reached for my stash of brown sugar. I took a pill out and tried to break the damn thing in half. I swallowed the entire pill, and then I stretched out on my bunk.

"Hey bro, I hope you're wrong. I hope you can get on with living your life."

"That would be nice. I'm bushed Leto. I need to check out."

"Me too, bro."

. . . .

Through a light fog, I try to figure out where I am. Then I realize
I'm just five blocks north of The Fourth Street Diner.

"How are you, Jack," said a familiar-looking guy standing on the
sidewalk smoking a cigarette. He looks familiar, but I can't recall
who he is. All I know for sure is his cigarette stinks. "Do I know
you?"

"You sure do. It's been a few years, but I haven't changed a bit.
You've changed, I recognized you even after all these years and the
damage the accident did to your face. You don't remember me," the
man answered as he dropped the cigarette butt on the sidewalk.
"I'm your dad. I'm out here because your mom and your sisters
are shopping in that store. You remember how I hated shopping,
don't you? It's amazing, being dead all these years, and I still hate
shopping."

"Dad, you look the same. Yes, I remember how much you hated
shopping. Oh my God, it's so wonderful to see you again."

"That's why I'm standing out here in the fog. I thought I'd come
out here and have a smoke."

"I can't believe I'm talking to you."

"Yep, that's me. I'm your father. You've grown up since the last
time I saw you. You've grown into such a great adult. Can I ask you
something?"

"Yeah, you can ask me anything."

"Why did you take the stand today? Most people on trial do not
take the stand."

"My lawyer did not want me to testify on my behalf, but I
insisted."

"Why?"

"I want the jury to hear my story from me. I don't want you to worry, but."

"Do you think the jury will acquit you?"

"No."

"I hope you're wrong, son. I'm sorry for the way things turned out for you, but regardless of how the trial turns out, I'm so damn proud of you. If you can stick around, your mom and your sisters will be out in a minute or two."

"Oh yeah, that's right Sara, Jane, and mom are in that store shopping?"

"I have to tell you son, you're looking good, I can't tell you how great it is to see you. How about joining your mom and sisters and I for a late lunch? That would be nice, we could all catch up. Would you like that?"

"Are you kidding? I love that. Hell yes, I'd love to have lunch with you. How's mom doing? When she died, she was in so much pain it was a blessing."

"Here they come, son. Why don't you ask her yourself?"

"Oh, my God. Jack is that you?" said my mother, dropping her purse and rushing over to me for a hug. She melted in my arms. Tears were flowing as she held on for dear life.

"Yeah mom, it sure is me. It's great to see you again. Are you in any pain?" Tears were streaming down everyone's faces.

It took a few seconds for my mom to compose herself, but she answered, "No, I feel fantastic."

"Aren't you going to ask about Jane and me?" my sister Sara questioned.

When I saw my sisters, I cried. Both my sisters cried, my mother started shedding tears, and my dad lit a cigarette. They were tears of pure joy as our entire family embraced on the sidewalk. I stepped back to get a look at my two beautiful sisters. "Look at you two. You're all grown up; you both look so beautiful."

"Tell us something we don't already know," said Jane, wiping her tears away. "Are you still pissed off at me because I caught the most fish up at Big Bear?"

"Jane, he's not upset at you," said Sara. "He's pissed at me. If you remember, I caught the biggest fish. If I remember correctly, I don't believe our brother caught a single fish. In fact, all he caught was a case of poison ivy. Jack the little pansy ass sissy boy."

"I still think you two are so moronic."

"I know you are but what are we," answered Jane again. She wiped tears from her face.

"All three of you behave yourselves," ordered my mother.

"Why don't we all go have lunch together?" asked my dad as he lit another cigarette.

"Oh my God," said my mother as she looked at her three children, tears streaming down her cheeks. "This is so wonderful."

"I know a place a few blocks from here if you want to go there. It's a cute little place called The Fourth Street Diner. It has great food and great service. In fact, I know the server, she's a friend of mine."

"It sounds like a great place to sit down and get caught up," said my father. "Which direction should we go?"

"Follow me Dad, the Fourth Street Diner is that way," I said as I pointed south.

I watched my parents walking together, holding hands, leading the way to the cafe. We followed like the children we once had been.

Sara whispered into Jane's ear. Both started laughing.

"What are you two up to?" I asked. "I still don't trust you!"

"Jane and I have an idea," answered Sara.

"What's your idea?" I asked.

Sara looked at Jane and smiled while we followed my parents and me to The Fourth Street Diner.

"Are you ready, Jane?"

"Let's do it."

Together they began.

"I wish I had a nickel,"

"I wish I had a dime,"

"I wish I had a boyfriend to kiss me all the time."

"My mom gave me a nickel,"

"My dad gave me a dime,"

"My sister gave me her boyfriend to kiss me all the time!"

"Even after all those years, I still can't stand that damn nursery rhyme. I told them to stop. We arrived at the cafe just after they finished. Something tells me they weren't too fond of the nursery rhyme either."

After we entered the cafe, my dad noticed a beautiful woman who kept looking in our direction. "Jack, do you know that woman over in the corner?"

"Maggie, I can't believe you're here. Would you like to meet my family?"

"On one condition."

"What?"

"First, I want a hug and a big smooch from you."

"Not a problem."

"Everyone this is Maggie Stewart, she's, my girlfriend."

"Maggie's infectious smile and her sweet personality impressed my family. Just as we sat down, my ex-wife and son walked in the cafe."

Judging by the look on my younger sister's face, she figured something was becoming weird! She leaned over and asked me who they were? I stood up and introduced my former wife Alison and my beautiful son Jake! I explained, just in case you were wondering, it was my fault.

"Hi dad," said Jake as I approached.

"Hello son," I answered as we hugged.

"Jack is this handsome man your son?" asked my dad as he walked up behind me.

"Jake," I said, "I'd like to introduce you to your grandfather."

"Nice to meet you," responded Jake as he extended his hand.

"Oh hell," said my father, "come here and give me a hug." My father gave Jake one of his famous bear hugs. "You're one handsome man. You realize that good looks and incredible charm runs in the family?"

"Dad, don't you see the resemblance between you two?" I said. "It's amazing."

My mother and sisters are talking to Alison and Maggie; they seem to get along just fine.

Olivia taps me on the back. "Jack, you need to get everyone to sit down so we can get your lunch order. Oh yeah, Jack, has the jury decided anything?"

"They just started deliberations after lunch today."

"Well, kiddo, I'm keeping my fingers crossed. I hope my testimony helped you. Is this going to be a single check, or is it going to be a royal pain in the ass for me?"

"Since I've been in the Marsh County Detention and I don't have a penny to my name, it will be separate checks."

"Well shit," answered Olivia, "you're lucky that we're friends, or I'd be cranky. Hold your horses, this is a dream, everything's on the house. What was I thinking? Jack, it's your job to get their asses in the chairs."

"I'll do it."

Chapter 26

Joe Hammer

"Let me guess," I said as Jackson Maynard sat down across the booth from me. "You've finally come to your senses and dropped your case against my client."

"No Joe, your guy is spending the rest of his life where he should be, in prison with zero chance of parole. I'm stunned by how quickly you've turned into a true defense attorney."

"Well, I've come to my senses. If you won't drop your ridiculous charges against my client, what was so urgent that you needed to see me?"

"I told you I'd get back with you if I heard anything about Eric Warren."

"Is the bastard going to jail?"

"Funny you should mention that. Over the past week there were rumors the state's bureau of investigation somehow received a video of my boss having fellatio with a young girl of questionable age at some swinger joint here in town."

"You're kidding?"

"I'm dead serious. They have evidence of the DA being blackmailed by the Sartori Family to get special consideration with some of their businesses and their associates."

"Is this true?" It took everything I had to contain myself. I feel a little vindicated that the bastard got caught. Maybe I can use this news to help Jack get acquitted.

"These state investigators are people no one wants poking around in their past. This morning three investigators came into our office unannounced and arrested Eric Warren. They handcuffed him, read him his rights, and took him out the front door. It was the most perfect case of poetic justice I'd ever seen. Guess who was waiting just outside our offices? The local media showed up and waited outside of

233

our office. They got Eric on video as they carted him off to the Marsh County Detention Center. Go figure! Make sure you watch the local news tonight. As we speak, he's being processed at the Marsh County Detention Center awaiting arraignment."

"Did all this happen this morning? Wow, it's always the damn holier than thou bible thumpers. Eric deserves everything that's coming his way. What about Dr. Stewart that your office has been protecting? Are you going to do something about that creep?"

"Are you talking about your client again?"

"Yep, it would be an excellent time to do the right thing and drop the charges against my client. You and I both know he didn't kill that woman. To go forward with this case is wrong."

"Joe, is your probation tied to an acquittal? You've done an amazing job of defending your client. You, of all people, should know how this works. Just so you don't think I'm a heartless bastard. We investigated. We didn't find a shred of evidence that shows your client is innocent. There's no evidence that made me suspect Maggie Stewart's husband. Our investigators checked both guys out. I already know how arrogant he is. If they arrested people for being arrogant they would have arrested you twenty years ago."

"That's a load of crap and you know it. You're forcing me to go after you. This isn't right and you know it."

"Well, Joe, maybe the jury will agree with you."

"Have you heard anything about how the jury's doing?" I asked.

"One bailiff told me the judge had a come to Jesus meeting with them, but he didn't say why. Your guess is as good as mine."

"I hope the jury exonerates my client."

"We'll find out soon."

"Yeah, that's for sure. I need to meet my client at the Marsh County Detention Center; I want to spend some time with him. I appreciate you telling me about Eric. It just occurred to me he is at the same detention center as my client. Hm, maybe I'll drop by and give him my card. I suspect he'll need a talented defense attorney."

• • • •

"Hi Jack," I said as the guard let me into the holding cell. "You brought me a grande latte, thank you Joe," said Jack on seeing I brought him his favorite coffee drink.

"How are you?"

"Under the circumstances, I'm doing okay. I wish this jury would decide and get this night mirror over. What's going on? Is everything okay?"

"Oh yeah, I thought you might enjoy some company. Just to break up your day. We need to go over some stuff before the jury finishes."

"Have you heard if the jury is making any progress?"

"I heard they are having heated debates. The rumor is Judge Taylor had a brief pep talk with the jury."

"Is that good or bad?"

"Neither. Some lawyers claim they know. If you ever have a lawyer that tells you something like that, fire them. They don't know what they're talking about."

"So, you don't know?"

"I've practiced law for over twenty years, and I can tell you this is the most grueling time. Guilty, innocent, or hung, it's in the jury's hands. It's anyone's guess. Let's go over some stuff."

"All right."

"The jury will find you innocent, guilty, or a hung jury. Those are the only options. If they find you innocent, then you and I go have dinner at The Fourth Street Diner, my treat. Have you made any plans where you can live until you get settled?"

"Not really."

"Don't you think it might be a good idea if you come up with something?"

"Joe, did you know the landlord at my old apartment confiscated everything I owned and sold it to pay for my back rent? They even got rid of all of my books. How chickenshit is that? There's hardly any value in used books."

"I'm sorry, Jack, how many books are you talking about?"

"Few, three-hundred fifty to four hundred, something like that."

"Oh wow? What books did you have?"

"I had all the published works of Wallace Stegner, Eudora Welty, Norman Maclean, John Grisham, Steven King, Laura Hillenbrand, and Harper Lee and a few others."

"Did you read all that stuff?"

"Why else would you buy a book? Some of those books I've read several times."

"Did your landlord get rid of them before I got involved with your defense?"

"I can't answer that. I received an eviction letter from the landlord and my belongings sold to pay part of my back rent. The letter quoted the state law, which gives them the legal right to confiscate my property to pay my outstanding debt. The letter also was a statement informing me I owed them around a thousand bucks and change."

"Do you have the letter?"

"It's in my cell."

"Give it to me, I'll contact them and find out what's going on. Is that okay with you?"

"Sounds great. Getting back to our conversation about the unlikely chance the jury finds me innocent. Olivia told me I could stay with her for a while. Martha said I could have a job doing dishes and cleaning the kitchen every evening. It's not much, but at least I'm not sleeping on a bench in Homestead Park."

"Can you get your old job back at the company you were working for before you got arrested?"

"I doubt it. Let's be honest, why are we discussing this? You and I both know there's no way in hell I'm getting acquitted."

"I don't know that and neither do you?"

Jack takes a drink of coffee, then fidgets in his chair. He takes several obvious nervous breaths. "Thank you for all the work you did on my behalf. I can't tell you how much it has meant to me. Many people told me about how big of a jerk you are, but I don't feel that way. I'm so lucky that you represented me. I don't think anyone could have done a better job."

"Thank you. It was my pleasure. I don't know for sure, but I think there's an excellent chance they will acquit you. Everyone knows they're bullshit charges. You are a friend. We come to appreciate each other. You'll do just fine."

"Joe, I know you mean well. I don't want to offend you, but deep down you know this is the end of the road for me regardless of the jury's decision. If it's a hung jury, the prosecutor will retry the case if for no other reason than to save face. If they find me guilty, I'll spend the rest of my life in prison. There is a one in a million chance the jury will acquit me, if that happens that's great. Then what do I do, Joe? I guess I'll go back to being a person living on the fringe."

"Did you ever think your attitude isn't helping you?"

"I understand Joe, but you're my lawyer when this is over. You will move on with your life and practice law. I think that's great for you. Circumstance threw us together, but we live in different realities. The America you live in is a lot different from the one I live in. How many countries do you know where a man running for President can mock a disabled reporter and still get elected? That facts show a lot about our cultural norms towards disabled people. Your America is about conformity. Every day, I get defined by my facial features. My features make most people uneasy. I don't see that changing soon. No one gives a damn about those of us who do not fit in. They don't take people who look like me seriously." Jack stops to take a drink of coffee. "America is about being just right. We landscape our lawns, carefully choose the type of car we drive, and insist on everything being just right, without exception. People spend all kinds of money on making themselves a little more presentable. I don't have the luxury of changing how I look. In this culture they see my face as something grotesque."

"Cry me a river, Jack. You don't believe all that whiney crap, do you?" I asked, knowing full well he was right.

"Pick a movie. How many times do the bad guys have disfigured faces? I'm not telling you this to get any sympathy."

"It's this way all over the world," I responded. "Some places are a lot worse than here."

"Joe, I don't live in those places, I live here. I hate to tell you this: we are not, and never have been, the shining city on the hill. That's just how it is, like it or not, it's in our DNA. We live in a country that until fifty years ago had, ugly laws, in cities across the country. People with a facial disfigurement are not welcome to be in public. It's hard to find a job and even harder keeping it. This is what I have in my future if I'm acquitted."

Not that I didn't believe him. The fact is, I know it's all too true. Jackson Maynard is doing to my client what I did when he was doing his job. Not one time did I look at it from my client's point of view. I had no idea how facial differences consumed every aspect of Jack's life. "I'm not disagreeing with you, it's too much to take in. Processing all of this is difficult. It's easier to dismiss it as bullshit. At least that way I don't have to grapple with it."

"I understand, Joe. There was an innuendo the prosecution used throughout the trial. What would a woman like Maggie Stewart have in common with a man who looks like me and has my history? Every aspect of the relationship between Maggie and I had come into question. We had nothing in common, except we had everything in common. Maggie was eye candy. Nothing more than a sexual conquest of the rich and famous. In our culture, being beautiful has many rewards, it also has a dark side. She paid a terrible price when powerful influential men manipulated her, tried to cheat her out of her money, and worst of all, being assaulted too many times while authorities look the other way. When Maggie was in the public eye, they subjected her to terrible treatment. Her beauty was as much of a curse to her as my facial disfigurement has been to me. Most people saw her as nothing more than a wealthy object, a great-looking piece of ass, a very fuckable broad. Every time Maggie and I ventured out in public, someone gawked at me, lusted after her, and wondered what the hell was going on. If I get acquitted, what do I have to look forward to, more of the same old shit? Maggie made my life something to look forward to. Maggie was Maggie, that's all she needed to be. We were in love."

I knew he was telling me his truth. A truth that had to be difficult for him to express. It was an uncomfortable truth for me to hear.

"I understand why people questioned the relationship Maggie, and I had. Olivia O'Toole threatened her because she didn't believe someone like her could fall for a guy like me. We were opposite sides of the same coin. Joe, you know, and I know I will not beat this. Tomorrow the jury will convict me, then I'll become a revenue stream for a private, for profit, prison system. That's what America has become."

"Jack, let's wait and see."

I listened to Jack's view of America. I understood what he'd been saying all along. There are two different versions of America. If only I had taken the time. The America where I live is a land of opportunity. The sky is the limit. A place where most of the benefits went to those with the right skin color, who loved the right person, had an acceptable ethnicity, who were able-bodied, and worshiped an acceptable religion. These are the people who had the chance to get an education and make a career. If they worked hard and followed the rules, they would prosper like nowhere else in the world. When America works, it's great. The trouble is that America fails too many people too often. We cast aside these people from cradle to grave, left unable to prosper or defend themselves.

I realized what Judge Horton said about the other, not so welcoming version of America. Where the justice system is a trap for those without the means. I knew all too well these people were the low-hanging fruit that young prosecutors, like me, used to further our careers and bolster our reputation for being tough on crime. It was what I had done for over twenty years.

Chapter 27

Come Away with Me

"Hey Jack, where ya been?"

"My lawyer wanted to talk to me," I answered as the guard removed my handcuffs. "Leto, what did you decide?"

We both remained quiet until the guard walked away.

"I'm taking a plea deal. Looks like I'm going in for two and a half to five years. Sentencing is tomorrow afternoon. I learned two lessons."

"What?"

"If I ever get out, I'm moving to a state where the pot is legal. Then trust me, even then I'll never sell pot to a red-headed freckle faced puto from the suburbs, even if it is legal. Do you have any idea how your jury is leaning?"

"No, everything is quiet. That's the worst thing about this whole trial."

"What are you going to do if they find you not guilty?"

"That's not going to be my problem. The only thing worse than a conviction might be an acquittal. I don't have a penny to my name. A friend of mine said she'd let me stay with her until I get back on my feet. The apartment complex where I lived sold all of my stuff, including all my books. All I have are the clothes on my back. Did I tell you about Olivia O'Toole?"

"Oh yeah, I think so, the old lady, right?"

"Yeah. She said I could stay in her apartment. I can have a job washing dishes and cleaning the cafe where she works. It's not much, but at least I'm not living over a sewer vent."

"That's true."

"Leto, I got to tell you I'm sorry you're going to prison, that sucks."

"Me too. They told me I'm going to Baker/Stanfield Facility, one of those, 'for profit prison' that will screw you over at no extra charge. Not too sure I'll ever get off for good behavior. If I go home early, they lose money. The asshole owners will never admit it, but when their goal is to make a profit, that is the most important thing there is. It doesn't matter if it's a donut shop, a hot dog stand, or a private for-profit prison, only one thing is important, making money. Everything else they tell you is total bullshit. That's why this place stinks like piss all the time."

"I suppose I'll end up in one of those places too."

"There's a rumor going around the cell block. Did you hear anything?"

"Nah, I didn't hear anything. I noticed the guards whispering to each other. That must be what they're talking about. What's the rumor?"

"They say some dude being processed got shanked at least ten times in the gut and twice in his throat. It all happened about an hour ago when he was in the shower," said a voice from the next cell. "Somebody wanted that bastard dead. I heard he was some kind of important dude."

"He ain't important no more," said another voice from across the corridor. "Don't know if it's true or not, but he was an important lawyer."

Leto laughed, "Well whoever he is, he's an unimportant dead lawyer now."

"Sometimes there is justice," I said, as I got ready for bed. I grabbed my stash of brown sugar pills and sat in the shadows of my cell for a few minutes, deciding what I should do. I put the pills back, then stared at them for several minutes, trying to decide.

"Are you nervous about the jury?" asked Leto.

"Yeah, I have to admit I don't know why. Maybe it's because I'm going to prison for the rest of my life."

· · · ·

"Good morning, Jack," said Joe as he took his seat at the defense table. "How ya holding up?"

"I'm okay, I guess. Have you heard anything one way or the other about the verdict?"

"We'll find out together in a couple of minutes," answered Joe.

The bailiff gets everyone's attention. "All rise, Department Nine of the Superior Court is now in session, Judge Diane Taylor presiding."

The bailiff opened the door for Judge Taylor. She takes her seat and whispers to one bailiff. The bailiff walks to the door and waits for the judge's signal. The judge is reading a document and making notes. A few people are still entering the courtroom at the last minute. Jackson Maynard and his second chair are sitting at the prosecution's table.

I watch the older bailiff escort the jury into the courtroom. As the jury is taking their seats, the prosecutors, my lawyer, and especially me are trying to read the faces of each of the jurors.

Judge Taylor looks up at the audience. "Good morning, ladies and gentlemen. We received word late last night that the jury came to a verdict. Is that right, madam foreperson?"

"Yes, your honor."

The bailiff walked over to the foreperson. She gave the bailiff the envelope. The bailiff took the envelope to the judge, who opened it and without expression read the verdict. "Before I ask the clerk to read the verdict, I must insist that the people in the audience refrain from reacting. It doesn't matter whether you agree or disagree with the verdict." The judge turns her attention to the foreperson. "Was it a unanimous decision?" asked Judge Taylor.

"Yes, it was unanimous," answered the foreperson.

"Good," said Judge Taylor as she gave the clerk the envelope, "you may read the verdict."

• • • •

A loud clanging sound interrupted the proceedings, demanding everyone's attention.

"Hey Holt, wake up!"

I woke up to see the silhouette of a guard standing at the door to my cell. The guard once again rattled the cell door, waking the entire cellblock from a dead sleep. It was a dream.

"Hey Holt, I thought you'd want to know that the jury came to a verdict."

I was only half awake. "I'm sorry, would you mind repeating that?"

"The jury came to a verdict," said the guard as he began walking away from their cell.

"What did they decide? Do you know?"

"Nope. We just found out about it a few minutes ago. The jury came to a verdict earlier this evening."

As I sat on my bunk, I wondered how to get back to sleep. Leto was already sound asleep. I began considering my options. I considered the remote possibility the jury would find me innocent. What the hell would I do if that happened? I'm screwed, no matter what the jury decides. What should I do? I hid my stash of brown sugar near my bunk. I sat on my bunk in the darkness of my cell I considering my options. Again, I stared at the brown sugar pills. I looked around at my surroundings for what seemed like forever. I don't know why, but I could smell the stench of urine. The pungent smell that consumed the entire jail I had somehow grown accustom. I thought about my son Jake, my ex-wife. They're living the life they deserve. I'm so proud of my son. He's such a great kid. Alison did such a wonderful job of raising him. In the shadows of my cell, I realize the last three brown sugar pills were in one hand a small bottle of water was in the other. My only option and all I want to do is spend the rest of time with Maggie.

. . . .

A thick layer of fog covered the cold, wet city streets, setting off a cacophony of colors from the neon signs. The shards of light shot through the fog like vibrant, multicolored miniature bolts of lightning. I'm no longer worried about how the jury finds me. I'm with the love of my life, Maggie.

"Dad?"

"Jake?" I can barely see him.

"Yeah dad, it's me, I just wanted to see you again."

"How nice. I don't think I told you I always loved you and I will always love you. Thanks to your mother, you turned out to be amazing. While I was around, I should have told you how much I love you. I was wrong. I'm sorry."

"Dad, no need to apologize, mom and Olivia explained everything. I wanted to see how you're doing. I heard the jury reached a verdict?"

"That's what I heard, too."

"Well?"

"Well, Jake, that's a damn good question. I wish I had an answer. I'll let you know when I hear. Where's your mom?"

"She went home to Portland to be with dad."

"Okay, please know Jake, no matter what happens with the trial or anything else, it will be fine. Your mom and dad did a great job of raising you."

"Dad, I just wanted to tell you I'm glad I got the chance to meet you."

"I'm glad to see you too. I wasn't much of a father, but that doesn't mean I didn't think about you every day."

"I understand. Dad, you need to go to The Fourth Street Diner before this fog gets too thick. Maggie is waiting for you."

"Are you leaving?"

"Yeah, I need to get going but not to worry, we'll have a lot more time to get acquainted."

"I love you, Jake."

"I love you too, dad!"

He vanished into the fog. The Fourth Street Diner wasn't far away. Even though it was a cold, damp night; I've never felt so warm and peaceful.

I saw Maggie sitting in our booth, drinking wine as if she was waiting for me. Before going inside, I couldn't help but stand on the sidewalk just out of her view, admiring her. She looked in my direction and gave me an odd look.

"Don't you look debonair this evening," said Maggie as I entered the diner. "You're as handsome as ever. Just so you know, I already ordered a Cabernet Sauvignon straight from the vineyards of Bordeaux. There are those who say the wine list here lacks a certain, how should I say, 'je ne sais quoi'. Trust me, Jack, I'm in love with you. To be with you in this little jewel of a cafe is more than anything I could have imagined."

"Thank you. The feeling is mutual. I can't tell you how happy I am."

"I've been waiting for you all of my life," said Maggie. "The fog looks like it's getting thicker by the minute. I was afraid you wouldn't make it. Before I forget, I made you a new friendship bracelet."

"There is no way I would miss the opportunity to be with you. There is no other place I'd rather be than with you. Thank you for the bracelet." I put the new friendship bracelet on my left wrist.

"Before you sit down, may I give you a smooch?"

"You never have to ask that question." She stood up and moved in for an embrace. "Give me a slobber of smooches. I love feeling your body next to mine."

"I was so afraid you wouldn't come here tonight," she whispered.

Remembering how her warm breath felt on my neck, the feel of her body next to mine. Without a word, Maggie stroked my face and stared into my eyes. I knew I was where I needed to be.

"Let's sit down and be with each other?" asked Maggie.

"I love you, Maggie." The two of us talked, cried, and laughed for the next hour. Drank a little wine, hoping the evening would never end. We held on to each other like we'd never let go. Nothing else mattered. We were together.

"Come away with me?" Maggie whispered. "I love you."

"I want to be with you forever."

We stood up once again and embraced. I helped her with her red silk scarf and her beige trench coat.

"Jack, Maggie," Olivia walked over to run her fingers through my hair, "You are such a lovely couple. I love you both."

As we approached the door, I could see the reflecting orange glow of the neon sign. We didn't have a care in the world.

"Jack, I'm so lucky to have found you."

"I love you, Maggie, with all my heart."

The beginning

The fog slowly consumed us as we went out into the darkness of the night. We stood beneath the orange glow of the neon sign, feeling the warmth of each other's embrace. I once again whispered to her how I'm crazy in love with her. We kissed again before the fog consumed us.

About the Author

We are all ultimately defined by the events in our lives I'm no exception. The first defining experience in my life was contracting Bulbar Polio at eighteen months of age. My second experience was being raised in Gilbert, Arizona, during the fifties and sixties. It was an idyllic Southwest community of mid-twentieth century American. The population was around 1800 people, including those who lived outside the city limits.

My wife (also a Gilbert girl) live in Marana, Arizona, a northwestern suburb of Tucson. She's also my best friend, my squeeze, doubles as my editor, and is my most ardent fan and my most vocal critique.